The Old Cotswold Dialect

Selected articles of Charles Gardiner

Introduction

In the late 1950s there was a brief pause in the (frustratingly) intermittent flow of Ben Judd's articles on Asum Grammar; a gap filled by a fascinating series of articles by Charles Gardiner on the 'Old Cotswold Dialect.' This booklet collects together these articles, adds notes and extras, and rounds it off with a glossary of bits and pieces.

Acknowledgements

Charles Gardiner wrote the articles on 'The Old Cotswold Dialect for the *Evesham Journal* and I must, in the first instance, thank the *Journal* and its editor for granting permission to re-publish the articles. Where an article was found in the back copies of the *Evesham Journal* held in Evesham Public Library, it appears with a date. Where an article was found elsewhere, it appears without a date. If I have missed any articles, please send me a copy and it will appear in any future revised version.

Copyright

Publisher

Vale of Evesham Historical Society
The Almonry Heritage Centre
Abbey Gate
Evesham
Worcestershire
WR11 4BG
United Kingdom

www.vehs.org.uk

Published December 2008
ISBN 978-0-9558487-3-5

THE FIFTEENTH CENTURY WAYSIDE CROSS, SAINTBURY, GLOS.

The Old Cotswold Dialect

Aspects of the old Cotswold Dialect (6th November 1959)

For the past seventy years, successive country writers have predicted the demise of the old Cotswold dialect. In "John Darke's Sojourn on the Cotswolds", published in 1890, the author S.S. Buckman observed:

> Old customs and modes of expression die hard; yet it can be foreseen that dialect – an existing monument of speech of our Anglo-Saxon forefathers – will disappear before the advance of the schoolmaster and universal education.

In the first edition of "A Cotswold Village", published in 1898, J. Arthur Gibbs was no more optimistic than Buckman, for he wrote:

> As for the old-fashioned Cotswold dialect, in twenty years' time it will be a thing of the past.

And in 1932, H.J. Massingham sighed in "Wold Without End":

> It's grim to see how the old tongue is passing.

Is the old-fashioned Cotswold dialect, as J. Arthur Gibbs called it, dying it? It has suffered varied assaults down the years, beginning with the introduction of compulsory education for all country children, followed by alien impacts during two world wars, industrialisation, the radio and television, to say nothing of films from Hollywood. Yet the Cotswold dialect can scarcely be dead when one hears today such words as *hoggery-maw*, *quammocking*, *underminded*, *all seroi*, *tabbering*, *onntitumps*, *caddling*, *mombly-yudded*, and a host of local words that have survived from Shakespeare's day.

On the other hand, nobody can deny that dialect speech on the Cotswolds is declining. Some words that I heard as a boy in the South Cotswolds have disappeared; although, when a word seems to have gone for ever, it reappears in conversation with a Cotswold native, and not necessarily an old one at that.

Yet by all the rules and the onslaughts mentioned above, the Cotswold dialect ought to be on its last legs. How then, has it managed to survive? In considering this question we must remember that dialect dies hard because it is an unconscious form of speech, hereditary in character, with its roots deep in the past. It has been handed down from one generation to another – not by books and records, but by actual speech from old to young. Being unconscious, it's therefore spontaneous.

Thus, a countryman who has acquired dialect at an early age, then dropped it after living for years away from his first home, when searching for words in moments of strain or excitement, draws on his unconscious vocabulary, and before he realises it, out comes his native dialect.

In the same way, few countrymen are inarticulate in ordinary conversation, although they would be tongue-tied if called upon to make a formal speech. Like the Greeks, the Cotswold native has a word for it. Some new people came into a Cotswold village, and in academic speech they would be referred to an *nouveaux riches*. But old Dan'l told me confidentially: "*If you axes me, master; they'm folk who've made a smartish bit o' money quick.*"

And so men who have only limited schooling can rattle away in a most entertaining fashion to someone with whom they are at ease. There's no searching for descriptive words or phrases: the Cotswold dialect supplies them all with a wealth of colour and subtle meaning often absent from standard English.

What I have noticed over the years, however, is considerable alteration in the local pronunciation and accent as distinct from dialect as language. South Cotswold speech is nothing like so broad as my recollection of it half-a-century ago, and this was confirmed when I had the privilege of reading a private manuscript by the late Mr. F.S. Garnick, of Cheltenham, who recorded in meticulous phonetic spelling the Cotswold speech as he heard it in the early part of this century.

Here, I would express my concern about the paucity of written records of contemporary Cotswold dialect as distinct from dictionaries and glossaries. The numerous recordings of dialect by the BBC and professional philologists in recent years, among which are oral records of elderly countrymen, are of immense value; but there is a limit to their retrospective worth; because even the speech of an octogenarian has probably been affected unconsciously by far-reaching changes taking place around him during the many years since he first acquired his native dialect.

So far as written records are concerned, the South Cotswolds are more fortunate than their northern neighbours. I have already mentioned "John Darke's Sojourn on the Cotswolds" and Gibb's "Cotswold Village," both of which contain scholarly records and examinations of South Cotswold speech. But the best record of it in that region is a minor classic written throughout in phonetic dialect and published in 1871 in Cirencester. It's called: "Roger Plowman's Excursion to London."[*] It's author preferred to remain anonymous; but he is believed to have been a village schoolmaster.

---

[*] In the original article the book is called "Roger Plowman's Excursion to London in Zurich of Sairey Jane." However, I've hunted for a book with this particular title, to no avail. A pamphlet with the name "Roger Plowman's Excursion to London" can readily be found, and is mentioned in Arthur Gibb's book. SBB

I can find nothing comparable in the North Cotswolds so far as these three books go until we come to Massingham's "Wold Without End," published in 1932. This book contains a number of stories in the dialect heard in and around Chipping Campden, and concludes with a glossary.

The broad aspects of the Cotswold dialect which have been raised in this introductory review will be considered in detail and supported by illustrations in later articles. I should add, however, that while the philological aspects of my subject will not be ignored, I shall approach it primarily as a practitioner and an ordinary countryman who is interested in his native speech and in the native humour which is inseparable from it.

The Old Cotswold Dialect: 'Sound Pictures' (20th November 1959)

Some dialect words are onomatopoeic. They imitate the sound of the thing that they mean, and can therefore be described as 'sound pictures.' A typical example of this kind of word in everyday language is *ping-pong* – the fore-runner of table tennis.

In dialect, this type of word has probably been invented originally by a sharp-witted countryman on the spur of the moment, used, by him and others on later occasions, and eventually absorbed by the local dialect.

I think of such words as *slosheting* – tramping through mud or melting snow; and *ki-yking*, applied to a dog that runs away howling after being routed in a fight or hit by an angry human. *Whim-wamming*, I have heard applied to a cyclist free-wheeling at speed down a steep hill.

Quammocking refers to the internal rumbling arising out of an upset stomach. "*I has some of the gaffer's new cider, and it soon set my stomach a-quammocking. Quammock! quammock 'a kept a-guing.*"

A chaffinch is called a *chink* because of its call, in the same way that the cockchafer beetle is known on the Cotswolds as a *humbuz*, because the noise it makes is like that of a distant 'plane. In the Vale of Evesham this insect is referred to as a *bobhowler*. When turned on its back the cockchafer beetle buzzes furiously in its desperate but unsuccessful efforts to right itself; hence the Vale expression "*as drunk as a bobhowler*," which explains itself if you know what a bobhowler is and how it behaves when it loses its equilibrium.

Knackle is used to describe the noise made by the clicking of ill-fitting dentures. I've heard a person wearing a noisy set of false teeth unkindly called "*old knackle-tith.*"

A colourful example of a sound picture in the Cotswold dialect is *cagmag* – a woman who nags. It is also used as a verb, such as: "*Poor old Joe; he was well-nigh cagmagged to dyuth!*" That wonderful Chipping Campden character, Jimmy Teapot, who was a confirmed bachelor, when asked why he had never married, replied with a twinkle in his eye, "*Women? They be cagmags.*" He snapped out the two syllables in a way which gave them a wealth of meaning.

A Cotswold villager was returning from the railway station after seeing off his mother-in-law following her prolonged stay at his home. He went into the local inn and downed his pint of cider with more than ordinary speed and relish, declaring: "*Her's a cagmagging underminded vixen, and I've just bin to the station to welcome her off.*"

Clack means loud and persistent talk, usually on the part of a woman. As an example, when a villager was asked, "*Which sister do you mean?*" the reply came, "*Why, her with the clack.*"

A CORNER IN THE DELIGHTFUL COTSWOLD VILLAGE OF BROAD CAMPDEN (CHIPPING CAMPDEN).

I recently had occasion to employ the expressive word *zig-zag*, common enough in ordinary conversation, and I thought of its use in the Cotswold dialect. Rarely in that speech is it heard as a verb, but usually as a noun. A car would not zig-zag up the road – it would go "*all of a zig-zag.*"

All of which reminds me of a story from Chipping Campden. It happened many years ago. A Campdonian, who used his bicycle for transport, had been spending an evening with a hospitable friend, and instead of his customary scrumpy he had been regaled with a home-made wine which came within the local classification of "*tanglefoot.*" In other words, it went to the feet while the head remained clear. The departing visitor decided to push his cycle rather than ride it and he discovered not only his lack of co-ordination in his lower limbs but a tendency for his bicycle, though firmly grasped, to develop wayward tendencies.

As the Campdonian and his machine pursued an erratic course up the High-street, a kindly policeman inquired, "Are you all right, Tom?" "*Yes, master: I be all right, to be sure,*" Tom replied. "*Tis this yur bike what's ockud. You see, when I got him out of the shed this afternoon, I oiled the front wheel, but forgot to oil the back 'un.*" Then he added brightly, "*That's what makes he go all of a zig-zag!*"

Cotswold Dialect: Standard words (4th December 1959)

Words are used in dialect with a meaning different from that which they convey in standard English.

In local speech, *logic* denotes bad language or abuse. A woman complained of her neighbours: "*I can't stand their filthy logic.*"

Comfortable is applied to an amiable person – someone easy to live with. Thus an elderly Cotswold man described his wife as "*a most comfortable 'ooman.*"

Menagerie is not a collection of wild animals, but a complicated contraption, equivalent to the modern description 'Heath Robinson.' *Geometry* is a ramshackle structure.

Quilt in dialect can either be a noun or a verb. In the latter case, a person with tonsillitis would complain: "*I can't quilt (swallow).*" A local toper was said to be able to drink a pint of cider *without a quilt*. The reference had nothing to do with bedclothes. The speaker meant that his thirsty friend could drain a pint mug while his Adam's apple remained stationary.

Charm is generally applied to a person's character or to a pleasing mixture of bird song. But in the Cotswold dialect it is used to describe a conflict of raucous sounds, or a cacophony. I remember a tenant complaining of a neighbouring family, each member of whom played a different musical instrument indifferently and sometimes practised simultaneously. He said, "*You have never heard such a charm.*" I've also heard the expression: "*Kicking up a charm.*"

Cant is usually associated with insincerity or a pretence of piety. On the Cotswolds (and in other country districts) it means gossip, and not necessarily ill-natured talk. Asked if her husband was home, a woman replied: "*No, not yet. I count he's too busy canting down in the village.*" By the way, note the use of the word *count* for 'surmise.'

Mortal means 'very' in dialect. For instance, "*Now that's mortal queer.*" A variant is *mortable* carrying less force than *mortal* and akin to 'rather.' For instance, "*It's mortable cheerful of a night down in the Green Dragon.*"

In the Cotswold dialect *rusty* also means 'rancid,' and is applied particularly to bacon, somewhat in the same way that *ropey* denotes cider that has deteriorated in quality.

Comical, in ordinary speech, is associated with comedy, mirth or fun; but on the Cotswold, a man suffering from an internal disorder would say: "*My stomach do feel comical.*" A woman observed of a neighbour who was temperamental and moody: "*He's very comical.*"

The word is used in yet another sense. I was motoring with a country friend when we passed a field in which Merino sheep were grazing. He remarked: "*Look at those comical sheep,*" meaning that they were very unusual in appearance and breed, and not funny in the accepted sense.

These shades of meaning of the same word are difficult to define, and vary between one village and another. To gain a precise impression one has to look at such words in relation to their context.

The Cotswold Dialect: Links with Shakespeare: words that still survive (18th December 1959)

Some Cotswold dialect words are very old and can be found in Shakespeare's plays, although their original meaning may have altered since the poet's day. Here are some examples:

Warn: summon to a meeting.

Backwarn: cancel such a summons.

Dout: put out, e.g. *"Dout the light."*

Mammet: a puppet. Present-day equivalent: *mommet* – a scarecrow. Some philologists believe this to be derived from Mahomet, who is associated with effigies.

Inchmeal: bit by bit.

Odds: (noun) difference; (verb) to alter. Thus the Cotswold man complaining of the arrival of official summer-time referred to *"this yur oddsing of the time."*

Fall (verb active): to *fall* instead of 'fell' a tree is still common use on the Cotswolds and in the Vale of Evesham.

Talent: 'talon,' e.g. *"She had claws like eagle's talents."*

Buckle: bend. *"The wheel of his bike (or the wing of his car) was buckled."*

Handkercher (or *hankercher*): is still applied to a handkerchief.

The Yellows (or *The Yellers*): jaundice.

Thriller (or *filler*): is the name given to the shaft-horse in a team as in Shakespeare's day. When four horses were ploughing single on heavy land on the Cotswolds before being superseded by tractors, they were described in this order: the foremost, in-the-lash, the body-hoss and the filler.

Filberds: filbert nuts, as in the 'The Tempest'

Mammock: to tear or knock to pieces, is occasionally heard

Orts: for leavings

Tice: for coax

Reneague: to renounce a job or revoke at cards. I've also heard in the latter case: *feneague*, which is a corruption.

Plash: pool

Twit: blab

The Cotswold countryman and his neighbours also retain the Shakespearian double negative and double superlative. "*Nor never shall!*" has become "*That I never wunt!*"

"*The most unkindest cut of all*" has its present counterpart in "*He's the most straightforwardest man in our village.*"

The use of *on* for "of" as in *proud on* ("Much Ado About Nothing") survives in dialect, such as "*Her thinks the world on him.*" The preposition *of* is frequently used instead of *with* on the Cotswolds and in the Vale of Evesham, e.g. "*I'm a fed up of him.*" But this is not a Shakespearian survival.

But much older than the Shakespearian examples given above are the Anglo-Saxon features that have come down to us in dialect, and particularly the plurals such as *housen* for houses. Rarely heard today, but within my recollection, are *mousen* for mice and *foxen* for foxes. I've seen *primrosen* for primroses and *flen* for fleas; but I cannot remember hearing these spoken.

Also of Anglo-Saxon origin are *we'm* for "we are"; *hern* (hers); *theirn* (theirs); and *yourn* (yours). It is clear that a local speech which includes these survivals down the centuries will still be an unconscionable time a-dying.

My earlier references to "*this yur oddsing of the time*" reminds me that official summer-time is still resented by many of the older generation of countryfolk. I recall a stubborn old lady in the South Cotswolds who refused throughout the remainder of her life to alter her clocks following the "change in the hour" in World War I. Of course she had to make adjustments to follow the habits of the community; but she proudly claimed: "*I allus goes by God's time, and not this new-fangled affair.*"

The temporary introduction of double summer-time during the second world war was the last straw. An elderly farm worked in a remote village on the hills had been accustomed to going to bed at 7 o'clock and rising at some unearthly hour, and he refused to alter his habits for Hitler's War or double summertime. One of his duties was to look after the poultry, and when the clock was put back two hours an angry old man complained during the long June days:

> "*Drat this yur new summer-time, master. Tyunt right ner fair ner just. I can't have me proper night's sleep 'cos I got to get up so early to shut up the fowl.*"

The Old Cotswold Dialect: Some local variants (1st January 1960)

The exact boundaries of the region popularly known at "The Cotswolds" have never been authoritatively defined; but such a large area extending from a point above Bath in the south to "The Quiet Woman Inn" beyond Chipping Norton in the north is bound to produce some local variants in dialect, although some words and phrases are common to the whole region. When we consider the finer points of pronunciation, rhythmic utterance and inflection, differences are observed even between neighbouring villages.

The level tones of the natives around Cirencester in the south differ from the rhythmic rise and fall and the light and shade revealed in the speech of the Campden folk as exemplified by Ned Larkin (Bill Payne) of "The Archers." The inhabitants of the Oxfordshire border villages between Stow-on-the-Wold and Kingham have a habit of raising the voice at the end of a phrase and of finishing a sentence, as it were, in mid-air. In his radio impressions of "Our Bill," F.H. Grisewood makes use of this local dialect. A remarkable resemblance to this type of speech exists in the village of North Littleton in the Vale of Evesham, although it now seems mainly confined to the older generation there.

This last qualification also applies to many of the Cotswold villages, for in the surviving dialect there is a growing tendency towards a standard pronunciation, and such a tendency is likely to increase with children travelling from their own villages to schools some distance away in which pupils from a number of parishes mingle.

The speech of Burford and the villages around it savours both of the Grisewood dialect and of the South Cotswold speech, with the latter predominant. Listen to Tom Forrest (Bob Arnold) of "The Archers," and you will follow what I mean.

In the villages at the head of the Stroud Valley there was, before the First World War, a distinct sing-song characteristic in the local speech, but quite different from the rise and fall of the voices of the Oxfordshire border villages. This feature has again been "ironed out" down the years.

Included in a little book published anonymously at Cirencester in 1870 are a few verses to illustrate the basis of South Cotswold dialect pronunciation, and here they are:

> *If thee true Gloucestershire would know,*
> *I'll tell thee how us allus zays 'un.*
> *Put 'I' for 'me' and 'a' for 'o'*
> *On every possible occasion.*

When in doubt, squeeze in a 'w' –
'Stwuns' not 'stones.' And don't vorget, zur,
That 'thee' must stand for 'thou' and 'you,'
'Her' for 'she' and vice versa.

Put 'v' for 'f'; for 's' put 'z,'
'Th' and 't' we change to 'd.'
Zo dry and kip this in thine yed,
And thou wilst talk as plain as we.

This southern formula does not, in general, apply to the North Cotswolds. For instance, the *v* for *f* is less noticeable in the North, and so is *z* for *s*, and *d* for *th* and *t*. Against this, in the North the insertion of *y* or *w* before a vowel is much more marked than in the South. We hear *kyat* for the southern "cat," and *kyart* for "cart." Again, the Campden man would say *we'm* for the Southerner's *we be*, and *you'm* instead of *you be*.

One rarely hears *bist* in the North, and the Southern *cassn't* is heard as *kyant*. These are broad differences, however, and it is unsafe to generalise over detail, except that anywhere in the region and in the neighbouring Vale of Evesham, one is likely to hear the expression, *Her don't like she!*, thus following the injunction in the second verse of the rhyme to put 'her' for 'she' and vice versa.

The interpolation of the superfluous *do* with a very short vowel sound, such as *I d'like* and *what I'd'mean* is very common in the South Cotswolds and in Wiltshire and Dorset. Throughout the Cotswolds we heard *whirlipool* for 'whirlpool,' and the additional 'i' is inserted with pleasing effect in such words as *whirliwind, eariwig, pitchipoll*, and even *primmi-rose* for 'primrose.'

A story widely told in the South Cotswolds before the First War related to the visit of a well-known local farmer to London. His rubicund face garnished with side-whiskers, his dialect and his clothes made it clear to everyone that he came from the deep country. He was, in fact, the cartoonist's dream of Varmer Giles. He was a big man withal, and possessed a very powerful voice. He claimed that he only had to step outside the kitchen door of his farmhouse to make himself heard at any point on his 500-acre farm, and nobody, least of all his workmen, contradicted him.

As Farmer Sam waited for his homeward train, a cheeky porter said to him: "How's the turmuts a-looking down they way, gaffer?" Like a shot the answer boomed across Paddington Station: *About as green as thee bist!*

'Chapel-Barn": Netherton

DISUSED CHURCH, NETHERTON.

(Drawn by B. C. Boulter)

The Old Cotswold Dialect: Going, Going... (15th January 1960)

I thought of describing the words and phrases to be discussed here as 'Bygones,' but the use of such an expression would be unwise, for just as one thinks a dialect word has gone for ever it bobs up again. There are some words, however, which I have not heard personally in conversation, though I have seen them in books and glossaries, since the First World War which brought so many drastic changes to the English countryside.

Before 1914, *nation* was a common word in the South Cotswolds. Its meaning was comparable with *moral* (very) in the North Cotswolds. A villager would say on a wintry morning, *Tis a nation cold blow.* Or a man would say to his wife, *I doo feel nation tired, missus.* Can it be that *nation* is an abbreviation of 'darnation'?

Snowl for a lump, usually of bread, is now rarely heard; nor is *fire-new*, which is probably a contraction of "fire-brand new," although years ago when a villager was first seen wearing a new suit his friends would ask facetiously, *Where's the fire?* This arose through the custom of selling cheaply clothes and other articles that had been salvaged from a fire at a warehouse or factory. These were passed on in job lots to local shopkeepers, who in turn sold them at reduced prices to customers who could not afford the standard article.

Anent (against) and *athert* (across) are not yet dead. *Leazing* (gleaning) is very rarely heard because the custom of gleaning in the cornfields by the poor folk of the village has ceased. Nowadays an open gate after harvest simply means that the last man out with a tractor neglected to shut it; whereas in earlier days it had important significance to the women and children as an indication from the farmer that they were free to go in and glean.

Twizzle means to turn about sharply or twist round rapidly. I've never heard it since I played conkers as a schoolboy. Then it was applied to a chestnut which, when hit, span round at speed on the end of its string.

Mizzle is another old word that I never hear now. A glossary would probably define it as "to disappear." But, like many dialect words, it has a much finer meaning than that. It infers a surreptitious disappearance, rather like that of Longfellow's Arabs who folded their tents and silently stole away.

Razzle – to run at the roots and throw up suckers, and *spreathed* – applied to roughness of the skin on the hands or face induced by very cold weather, are rare, as is *zog* (to soak) and *spurtle* (to sprinkle).

Ruggle, which broadly means "wriggle," I've not heard since 1914 other than in a Mummer's Play.

Yoppeting (hounds in full cry after their quarry); *loppeting* (applied to a hare hopping leisurely); *scort* (to hurry); *dummle* (comatose, and used particularly in connection with wasps that lie about dopey at the end of the season) are rarities nowadays.

Miffy (offended); *maunder* (wander in one's mind and akin to momble); *blizzy* (nothing to do with a blizzard, but used in connection with a fire out of control, such as one in a thatched roof) are all going.

Then there are the picturesque words and expressions such as 'one-armed sailor' for a pump, and a 'lie-by' for a bed-fellow. I last heard the latter when a Cotswold woman tramp who for years had a male companion on her journeys said tearfully on his death, "I've lost my lie-by".

Out-asked (after the banns have been called for the third time); *will-gill* for an effeminate man, and *weeny* for a woman of indeterminate sex are virtually bygones.

Bat-fowling (used by Shakespeare in "The Tempest") is only heard in the reminiscences of elderly folk because this business of beating hedges at night and catching the disturbed birds in a net has long since ceased.

Zany for "simple" is very rarely heard, but its equivalents *sawney* and *yawney* survive. I've found from long experience, however, that many a villager who is described as *sawney* or as a *yawney* is more artful than daft, and it is most unwise to underestimate him.

A middle-aged single man in a Cotswold village came into a bit of money and proceeded to build what was obviously going to be a shop. He was looked upon not only as eccentric but simple. But even when nearly completed the building gave no indication of the nature of the business that was to be carried on, and the owner was reticent on the subject. A village gossip whose inordinate interest in other people's affairs was only equalled by a disinclination to pay her bills, decided to find out. "What sort of shop is this going to be, Mr. M.?" she asked, and received the solemn reply, "I'm afraid it wouldn't interest you, Mrs. Smith. This is going to be a cash store."

The Old Cotswold Dialect: Where do these words come from? (29th January 1960)

Looking at some of our outlandish dialect words and phrases, one frequently asks, "Where on earth do they come from?" Trying to trace the derivation of such words is fascinating, although I fear in many cases the conclusion reached is largely based on speculation.

Hoggerymaw, used as a noun, is a tool for trimming ricks, but it is so called defeats me. On the other hand, when a village carpenter says to his son or apprentice, *Don't hoggerymaw it about like that!*, we know that he is referring to a rough and ready approach to the job in hand which offends him as a skilled craftsman. Somewhat similar in meaning to *hoggerymaw* is *hox* – to hack or cut in a very rough fashion. *All seroi* can be traced, for it means "like a king." A person would say of a man sitting at a table obviously enjoying a good meal, *Ah! There he is, a-setting all seroi.*

Gawmed means sticky with mud. A countryman working on heavy land would say of his boots, *I got 'em all gawmed up.* This word probably springs from "gum."

Tabber (to drum with one's fingers) I heard used by a Cotswold villager who hired a taxi in London, the driver of which overran the place where his passenger wanted to stop. Describing the journey, the villager said afterwards: *I kept a-tabbering on the winder; but still he 'udn't stop.* Driving rain beating on a window or rattling on a galvanised iron roof attracts the word *tabbering*, which I imagine comes from the biblical drum known as the tabor.

The origins of *lear* (hungry); and *nineter* which is applied to a young boy who is a proper little rascal (an alternative being *erk* or *irk*) defy me.

Carney for artful of knowing; *hullocking* (big and awkward); *daddocky* (decayed); and *collogue* (to confer confidentially or quietly in a corner) are difficult to trace.

Bejade for tire and *misbecall* for revile or slander are plain alternatives for the standard words, and a woman is probably called *a proper old besom* because this sort of broom is associated with witches. Then there are the corruptions such as *sour as varges* for verjuice. But why *lozengers* instead of lozenges, and *sausengers* for sausages? I can, however, understand the pictorial description of *a master pair of dew-cutters* being applied to a man possessing very large splay feet.

I can only think that the double-blank in dominoes is called *Lady Godiva* because, like the Lady of Coventry, it is bare. On the other hand, why is a large pocket watched called a *turnip*?

Some dialect expressions are biblical in origin, such as *never in the reign of Sam!* A job which consists of a complete sinecure is called *a proper Solomon*, the inference being, I suppose, that all Solomon had to do was to sit and express opinions or pass judgement, as distinct from doing physical work. This reminds me that among an earlier generation the word *work* related solely to manual labour and anyone engaged in a clerical or professional capacity was in *a proper Solomon*, no matter how heavy his responsibilities. This contempt for non-manual work still survives among an older generation of country folk, and particularly in the Vale of Evesham.

A young man who was expected to take over his father's market garden preferred to do in for fruit and vegetable dealing and undoubtedly made a far better income that way. But, when someone called at his home to ask where he could be found, his mother said sourly, *He's gone into Evesham a-spivving.* This is a modern example of the way in which modern slang gets mixed with the local dialect.

I shall be delighted, however, if someone can tell me the origin of *carrying the grindstone*. I heard it applied, some years ago, to a village roadman in a detached community who invariably undertook the task of running to inform the midwife in a neighbouring village (before district nurses were on the phone) of an imminent confinement. I was told, *Yes, old Dan was a master good covey for carrying the grindstone.*

To conclude, I hark back to Lady Godiva, concerning whom a good story arose some thirty years ago in a North Cotswold village overlooking the Warwickshire plain. A most ambitious historical pageant had been arranged in Coventry, a feature of which was Lady Godiva riding through the city streets. Her nakedness, however, was protected by tights and enormous tresses to avoid offence to the most prudish alderman. A coach trip had been arranged to run to the city from the village and it was being discussed by two elderly natives on their allotments.

Going to the pageant a-Sattudy, Tom? asked Sam. *No; I think not,* was the reply. *I reckon I'll stay at home and get my taters up.*

Ah, but you ought to go, Tom, his friend urged. *There'll be a master procession, a capital good firework display and what not, and you can ride in that there big motor as comfortable as a biddy.*

Tom was still unimpressed. *No; we got to make the most of the weather, and I wants these yur taters home and dry.*

Sam made his final appear, earnestly and confidentially, *But you don't know what you'm missing, Sam. There's going to be naked 'ooman on a white hoss!*

Tom drove his fork into the ground after the manner of allotment holders, declaring seriously, *In that case, I shall go. I an't sin a white hoss this long time.*

THE ROLLRIGHT STONES, LITTLE ROLLRIGHT.

The Old Cotswold Dialect: Birds, beasts and flowers (12th February 1960)

The words given to birds, beasts and flowers form one of the most pleasing aspects of dialect speech. Snowdrops are *Candlemas bells*; the hemlock is known as *kecksies*; the wild arum as the *cow and calf*; the common flag as the *sag-iris*; and the wild fritillary found in the meadows in the South Cotswolds is called the *snake's head*, which is a good description of it.

When the Cotswold native is talking to his friends; the hedgehog becomes an *urchin* or occasionally the *fuzman pig*; a mole is an *oont* and its little mounds are called *oontitumps*.

A bumble bee is a *humbledore* and the cockchafer beetle a *humbuz* or a *bobhowler*. Ants are *emmets* or *pissants*; woodlice are *church pigs*; ladybirds are *flying cows*; the moorhen is a *dabchick*; the owl a *Povey*; the nightingale the *woodwail*; and although now rarely heard, the robin is the *ruddock*.

The description of the missel-thrush as the *storm-cock* is by no means confined to the Cotswolds; nor is the dialect name of *chink* for the chaffinch, derived from its thin little call.

Closely associated with the birds and the beasts is the weather, which attracts many dialect words and expressions. When the weather is changeable, it's *casualty*; if it's muggy, it's *pothery* or *puthery*; and when it's downright bad, it's *unkid*.

A *peffle* of snow is used to describe a few flakes falling lightly, whereas a *whiffle* indicates that the wind is driving them.

A cold searching breeze is called a *lazy wind* because, as a native would say, *it 'ud sooner go through 'ee than round 'ee!*

A bird inspiring a number of picturesque names is that handsome fellow – the green woodpecker. It is known in turn as the *yaffle* (or *yoffle*); the *woodsprite*; *laughing Betsy*; and the *eckle* which appears to be derived from *hecco*, for 300 years ago Michael Drayton (a poet with Cotswold associations) referred to "the sharp nebbed hecco stabbing at his brain."

Finally, in the South Cotswolds, the green woodpecker used to be commonly referred to as the *lawyer bird*, perhaps because of its knowing expression and long bill!

Here area few verses written eighty years ago in the local dialect, entitled "The Hornet and the Beetle," concluding with a warning as to the dangers of hasty litigation:

The Hornet set in an 'oller tree,
And a proper spiteful toad were he;
And he merrily sung while he set,
His sting was as sharp as a bayonet.
"Now who's so bold and fierce as I?
I fears not bee nor wopse nor fly."

A Beetle up thick tree did climb,
And scornfully did look at him.
Sez he, "Sir Hornet, who gave thee
A right to set in thick thur tree?
Although thee sings so nation fine,
I tell 'ee – 'tis a house of mine."

The Hornet's conscience felt a twinge,
But growing bold with his long sting,
He said, "'Tis plain for all to see,
I'm finer far than wopse or bee:
Be off, and leave the tree to me.
The mixen's good enow for thee."

Just then a Yoffle passing by
Was axed by them their cause to try.
"Ha! Ha! It's nation plain," sez he,
"They'll make a famous munch for me."
His bill was sharp, his stummick lear,
So up he snapped the caddling pair.

All you as be to law inclined,
This little story bear in mind,
For if to law you ever go
You'll find they allus serve 'ee so.
You'll meet the fate of these yur two:
They'll take your coat and carcass too.

The Old Cotswold Dialect: A Mixed Bag (26th February 1960)

I want to gather here a few interesting words which have not been included under previous headings. Some of them convey a fine shade of meaning difficult to interpret in standard English. Take *mawzy* which, as an adjective, can be used instead of *sleepy* for apples or pears beginning to go rotten inside. But it can also be employed as a verb, and as such, it provides a good example of my reference to fine shades of meaning.

An elderly Cotswold woman said of her late husband, who had very little to leave when he died, *He mawzed all his money away on hoss racing and they there football coupons*. Now she meant something different from "frittered away." The process which she had in mind was one of almost imperceptible diminution or whittling away, and like certain words in a foreign tongue, there is no precise translation to be found.

Then there is the dialect word of wide and varied application, like *nesh* or *nelsh*, which broadly means "weak." It is used to describe the stalks of corn that cannot stand up to the weather and result in the crop being "laid" by the first strong wind or thunderstorm. Yet it can be used to describe coal that gives out little heat when burning and, in fact, anything that lacks "body."

So far as individual words are concerned, it is impossible to give more than random samples, and I would like to add such interesting and picturesque words as *mugglement* (indicating confusion or a puzzling situation); *hockling* applied to an elderly inhabitant afflicted with rheumatism walking awkwardly or painfully with a stick, e.g., *I sin old Gramp a-hockling down the village street this morning*.

He fell mumpus, is used when a man fall flag on his back, and is different from *he fell all of a yup* (heap). *Scrump* – to eat with relish – is much older than the modern slang "scrumptious," and the association is probably quite accidental. *Gallus* meaning cunning of artful; but I've heard the expression, *it was gallus easy*, which means "it was just too easy for words."

Brevit is a good old Cotswold word and it infers searching or poking about, and is often used in an uncomplimentary way. One hears the expression *on the brevit* as distinct from *breviting about*.

Womble – to move awkwardly – and *wimbly* for "weak," whether of a human being or a plant are pleasingly descriptive. Their opposite is *sprack* for lively and vigorous. *Dan'l may be eighty years old, but he's as sprack as some of the young 'uns*. In a literary reference a man rolling home drunk would be said to be "wearing his crooked stockings." But on the Cotswolds we should say *he had a smartish wobble on*.

A *late-hatched 'un* describes a child born late in married life, usually after a considerable gap between the previous child or children.

A long dog relates to a fast-moving dog such as a greyhound and is used to illustrate a man running or proceeding as fast as possible, such as *I scorts down the hill like a long dog.*

Chunter means to converse in a quiet and friendly manner as would happen in the case of a group of old cronies sitting round the fire in the village inn and is different from *collogue* which infers some secrecy or even conspiracy. *Shackles* means "broth" or "soup" with a suggestion of a weak or watery concoction.

When a situation is *all Sir Garnet* we understand that "everything's OK." But why Sir Garnet? Does this refer to Sir Garnet Wolseley, the successful British soldier? By the way, Garnet is a common name in the North Cotswolds among the older generation.

We must not forget the common mispronunciations (as distinct from malapropisms) like *cantankertous* for "cantankerous"; *loo-warm* for "luke-warm"; and *obstropolous* for "obstreperous."

Further individual words that come to mind are: *clemmed* for that choking feeling that accompanies a severe cough; *skew-whiff* which means sideways or out of place, e.g. *Boy! Your cap's on all skew-whiff!*

Famelled is common for "starved" and no doubt springs from "famished." *Frit* is a plain abbreviated of "frightened," just as *frez* is a contraction of "frozen." *Dizen* for "bedeck" is pleasing, but now rarely heard.

Another word worth close examination is *underminded*, which a glossary would define as "mean." But it has a more oblique meaning than that. In my conception of this dialect word a person who is *underminded* is one who attributes to others the mean motives which he himself displays.

The Old Cotswold Dialect: Writing dialect (18th March 1960)

Writing dialect presents problems of its own, for when all is said and done, dialect is primarily meant to be heard – not read. On the other hand, the written word is still an important medium of communication and record. How then, can dialect best be recorded in narrative form as distinct from the dictionary and the glossary?

In writing dialect the author must consider for whom his work is intended. If the prospective reader is a student or someone with a special interest, then careful phonetic spelling can be employed. But, as Ben Judd explained in one of his expositions concerning the famous 'Asum Grammar,' there are serious difficulties in the way of producing in the printed page the various phonetic signs to indicate the exact pronunciation of a local word. It is impossible to translate into ordinary writing the exact sound of certain dialectic words, and little can be done to indicate the intonation and rise and fall of the speaker's voice. These cadences are an important feature of local speech, especially on the Cotswolds.

In dealing with the general reader of country books, magazines and local newspapers, I reached the conclusion that meticulous spelling in dialect narration (as distinct from an examination of individual words) becomes irksome to the reader even if he is acquainted with the particular local speech. Moreover, I feel that dialect should be presented in such a form that it can be understood by the general reader without recourse to a glossary or even footnotes, other than in the case of uncommon words. Not that I reject phonetic spelling entirely, for used judiciously it can certainly add colour and authenticity to the narrative. I never write *Oi* for 'I,' and very rarely do I indicate the dropped aspirate. Most important are natural rhythm and authentic idiom.

Most of my dialect writing has been done for radio and stage plays and for country speakers to broadcast. A mistake that I made in the early days was overdoing the phonetic spelling in scripts for talks, plays and documentary features. Over 20 years ago a BBC producer and I discussed this problem, and decided to try out our theory on an intelligent Cotswold farm carter who was appearing in a feature programme. We gave him his 'piece' in standard English; then told him to take it home and rewrite it just as he'd say it to a friend or in the local inn. When we saw his revised version we were surprised to see how little it differed from the original. Although he had altered such words as 'frozen' to *frez*, 'frightened' to *frit* and 'something' to *summat*, for the most part the standard spelling had been retained.

But this is the important point: when he came to read it to us, 'again' was pronounced *agyun*; 'week' became *wick*, and 'cart' was *kyart*. A valuable lesson was learned here, and I applied it in particular to broadcast drama, leaving experienced local amateurs to convert their lines into pure dialect. I think it also wise, when writing anything of length containing dialect words, to adopt a consistent method of spelling throughout.

Having been given the foregoing precepts the reader is entitled to ask for an example – so here goes! This story goes back to wartime days, and it was recounted by an aged inhabitant who spoke in the broadest Cotswold dialect. By the way, it is a good example of the manner in which the native, when recalling a conversation, attributes dialect to the parson, the squire or anyone who never speaks other than in the best English!

Tother marning I was setting outside The Dragon having me bit o' sunshine, when who should come up but the young squire who was home on leaf. I could see as he was just a nordinary private when he might easy have bin a colonel or general or summat high up with all he got behind him.

"Marning, Dan'l," he sez, "And how be you today?"

I sez, "I be proper middling, sir; and that's the certain truth."

He sez, "You come in yur along of I,"' and so I did. And he sez to the landlord, "Dan'l yur be proper middling. Draw him a double whiskey."

You should a sin it. Well nigh half-way up the glass it were. I sez, "If I drinks that, sir, I shall be mombly-yudded till Satudy fortnit."

He sez, "You get it down'ee; it 'ull do 'ee good."

So I did, and I can tell 'ee it warmed me up smartish, 'cos I most generally drinks nothing but scrumpy or crafty.

As we was a-going he sez, "How d'you feel now, Dan'l?"

I sez, "'Tis mortal queer, sir; but I be as right as trivit!" Now that's what I calls a proper genulmon.

The Yubberton Yawnies

Abridged from an article in the Evesham Journal (25th March 1976)

Abridged from an article in the Evesham Journal (25th March 1976)

Many tall stories are told about Ebrington, or 'Yubberton' as it known locally. Before his death in 1874, Jack Wheatcroft, was who born in the village, wrote some of these tales down on paper.

Ebrington, like so many small villages, has many a quaint story attached to it. Here they mucked the church tower to make it grow – being, so we are informed, jealous of the fine tower of their neighbours at Chipping Campden. They also enclosed the cuckoo in hurdles so that it would remain summer all the year long.

Should it become known that you come from Ebrington, then nine times out of ten the listener's mouth will curl into a smile when he realises you are a Yubberton Yawnie.

> *Yubberton Yawnies went to plough*
> *When they got there they didn't know how:*
> *They tied their horses to a stake*
> *And off they went to Willersey Wake.*

Sid Stanley's fire was an event not soon forgotten, it happened this way. Each village made a contribution towards a fund for maintaining a fire engine, this machine to be stationed at Blockley some three miles from Ebrington. Brick dams were erected in the brook in the centre of the village to maintain a supply of water if an when needed. Now time went by with no fire in the village, and it seemed a waste of money when we could not see the fire engine working. Then, oh joy! Stanley's barn, full or corn, was blazing merrily.

The villagers formed a chain to pass buckets from hand to hand while they waited for the arrival of the fire engine. Our excitement was intense as the vehicle drew into the yard and the firemen, all sit and polish, jumped smartly out and proceeded to unroll the hoses until reaching the dam.

They then discovered that the whole dam had been neglected and was silted up, full of mud and rubbish but no water. The firemen started rolling up their hoses, swearing at everyone and everything, and the villagers replied in Yubbertonian style. By this time, one and all had downed buckets, leaving the fire to itself.

Now this sort of affair could not be allowed to happen in future. A meeting was called in the schoolroom and suggestions asked for. At least, after much head-scratching, a certain farmer raised his hand and said: "Please, Mr. Chairman, I propose that in future, the dam is cleaned out the day before a fire!"

Mouse tails ½d. Rat tails 1d. Queen wasps 1d. These prices were paid in an attempt to improve crops, so all schoolchildren were busy poking into likely holes or chasing wasps. Threshing was in progress in the dutch barn and Sam agreed to pay these prices. After an hour or two's slaughter, quite a bundle of tail had been gathered and the lads decided to cash in on the kill. After the count had been taken and the wages paid, Sam says: "*Now back yu guz and kill some mo-wer*", and threw the tails into the muckyard. Fatal mistake! The boys' eyes had been glued on him to see what he would do with the tails and – yes, you've guessed it! – they were all presented to him again later in the day. "*My eyes!*" said Sam. "*You bu-oys yunt arf doin well!*"

There was also the case of a cherry picker with a spare ladder beside him. The farmer arrived on the scene, not in a good humour by any means. Glaring at the picker he shouted: "*No wonder we aan't got arf anuf ladders to gu round. What the 'ell are you doing with two on 'em?*" And from aloft came the quiet reply: "*Co-orse I wants two ruddy ladders! I wants one to get up and t'other to come down, do-unt I?*" The farmer grabbed the spare ladder, at the same time grumbling: "*I might a knowed, talking to a Yubberton bloke!*"

A Mare's Egg: Extravagant tale from Yubberton (12th November 1965)

'A mare's nest' was a common expression among Victorian politicians, and it is still occasionally used by elderly aldermen. But *A Mare's Egg* is something different. It is in the same category as 'Pigeon's Milk,' and its meaning is known only to a handful of Cotswold folk.

Now this story goes back a good many years when a Yubberton man named Bill had an allotment in a field adjoining the road leading from Ebrington towards Campden Station. In a way, Bill was the last of his line, for he cultivated his strip of land with that primitive agricultural implement known as the breast-plough which he used with skill and extraordinary speed. He could sometimes be seen carrying a bucket of water to his allotment – not, as one would imagine, to meet the needs of the few head of poultry that he kept there; but, according to his neighbours, to cool down the blade of his breast-plough which was liable to become red-hot when Bill decided to accelerate.

Having ploughed and skimmed his land, Bill gave though to his cropping programme, and looking at a fertile corner which was "in the furrow," he said to himself. "*I reckon I'll grow me a fyow pumpkins.*" The seeds that Bill planted prospered and, in due course, produced a crop of small, medium-sized and large pumpkins among which was one that dwarfed the rest. But although this giant was a source of pride to Bill, it became a problem. Housewives were ready to take any pumpkin of reasonable size which they stuffed and cooked after the manner of vegetable marrows; but nobody wanted one which was described by the other allotment holders as *"the masterest pumpkin as ever a mon did see."*

Bill's pumpkins were harvested in due course with the exception of *"the exter big 'un."* There it lay, in solitary state, until an early frost compelled Bill to pull out his pocket knife and sever it from the main stem. He put it under his arm and mombled thoughtfully towards the roadside gate.

An allotment holder who had grown a similar specimen a few years earlier, cut it through the middle, scraped out its contents, and used one part as a kennel for his dog and the other as a beehive. Bill had no dog and he hated bees. If he had been on good terms with the parson he could have made the pumpkin his contribution to the harvest festival, and had he lived elsewhere he might have put it on display in the bar of the village inn. At 'The Ebrington Arms,' however, neither the landlord nor the company encouraged such showing off by individual customers.

It so happened at this particular time that Uriah and Enoch, two young fellows from the Black Country, were spending the day with their granny at Ebrington. Granny was a kind old soul and, having entertained her guests with traditional country hospitality rounded off with a glass of her parsnip wine, she set them on the road to the station. After leaving the village, Uriah and Enoch observed a man standing in a gateway holding a strange spherical object.

"What in t'hell be that?" said Enoch. "Why not axe him and find out?" suggested his practical brother. Bill's reply to Enoch's inquiry was prompt and solemn. *"This yur be a mare's egg,"* he said. As the result of the conversation which followed, Bill parted with his ovoid marvel for a shilling.

Although showing no outward sign of pleasure, Bill was secretly delighted. He had rid himself of an encumbrance and he was a shilling better off in the process. Moreover, when the standard agricultural wage was thirty bob a week, a shilling was no mean coin of a realm.

Meanwhile, time was running out, and with Enoch carrying his awkward burden the Black Country pair stepped out smartly to catch their train. As they hurried down the slope towards Campden Station, the inevitable happened. The alleged mare's egg slipped from Enoch's grasp and rolled into some undergrowth at the side of the road. This disturbed a hare which went loppeting down the road closely pursued by the two men from Gornal shouting excitedly: "Hey! Stop our foal! Stop our foal!"

EBRINGTON, GLOS.

The Old Cotswold Dialect: Words from correspondents (1st April 1960)

My previous articles have resulted in letters and personal conversations in the course of which I have been asked question or reminded of individual words or aspects of the Cotswold dialect not hitherto mentioned. Some of my Chipping Campden friends go further than most: they order me on no account to leave out this word or that; but I have to explain to them and other readers that I cannot hope to do more than scratch the surface of the wealth of dialect material still to be found on *they there hills*. On the other hand, there are omissions to be repaired.

My first correspondent, an acquaintance whom I have not seen for some time and who lives away from Evesham, wrote to me saying that he had noticed one of my articles in a copy of "The Evesham Journal" which had been used to wrap up a purchase from his greengrocer. Here was an example of the long arm of coincidence and also a corrective to authors who have an exaggerated idea of the value of their work!

Anyway, he questioned my interpretation of the word *cagmag* which, in his experience as a Shropshire lad, had always been used in connection with tough or inferior meat unsuitable for human consumption. The word is, in fact, used throughout the Midlands in that connection, but the Cotswold *cagmag* (a nagging woman, or as a verb, to nag) is onomatopoeic and has no associated with the word employed in the meat trade.

A word common in Chipping Campden, which I have been asked to deal with more fully than in a previous passing reference, is *momble*. Apart from the adjective *mombly* (confused) and the expression *mombly-yudded*, it is used as an alternative to 'saunter.' For instance, *I was mombling up the street this morning when I sin old Garnet*. Better still, there is the story of the Campdonian who went to London on a day's excursion and became detached from the main party. His friends said, *Old Tom's mombled off and got hisself lost*.

Against the single word which has varying shades of meaning according to its context, we find a group of words meaning more or less the same ting, such as *thrape*, *larrup* and *jacket*, all verbs meaning "to beat." A South Cotswold native would say of an unruly boy, *the young varmint wants a good jacketing*. I mentioned in an earlier instalment that the local pronunciation of some Cotswold words defies the most careful phonetic spelling. *Thrape* (although it only has one syllable) is an example of this.

Local dialects are noted for their picturesque descriptive words and phrases and I am reminded of *Jack-above-Ground* for a very short man, and *Johnny-come-fortnit* for a packman or travelling credit draper.

For some years past a North Cotswold villager has sent me, from time to time, local words and dialect expressions which he still hears. *Dummle* or *dumble* (previously mentioned) is usually applied to comatose insects or dense individuals; but my correspondent recently heard it used in connection with the blunt edge of a tool that needed sharpening.

His example was: *This yur axe be dummle*. He has also heard recently, *Her would have classumed* (grabbed or appropriated) *the lot, but I likes things a bit ayzum-jaysum*. This last means 'above board' or 'upright and straight-down.' Here I would add that while some of these words and expressions are regularly used by individual Cotswold folk, they are no longer commonly used.

Several of my previous contributions have concluded with a Cotswold anecdote in light vein, and it seems that this is now expected as a tail-piece to every article of mine. On a sunny afternoon a tourist entering a small Cotswold town approached one of those elderly natives who can usually be found alone or with cronies at some vantage point, and knowing nothing of the poet, nevertheless subscribe in practice to the view of W.H. Davies:

A poor life this, if full of care
We have no time to stand and stare.

The visitor said to one of these Cotswold characters. "Tell me, please, my good man, which are the places of local interest in this beautiful old town?" only to receive the solemn reply, *There be five, sir; but they don't open till six o'clock.*

The Old Cotswold Dialect: Words from correspondents (15th April 1960)

My correspondents range from the graduate with an academic interest in the derivation of dialect words and their association with languages other than English, to the villager who has a keen interest in his native speech but finds it difficult to express himself in writing. In discussing some of the comments reaching me I have to remind readers of what I said in my introductory article – that I intended to approach my subject "primarily as a practitioner and an ordinary countryman interested in his native speech and in the native humour that is inseparable from it."

Nevertheless, I am pleased to hear from a correspondent who formerly lived on the Cotswolds that *leer* or *lear* (empty or hungry) occurs in Flemish, German and Dutch. *Hullocking* (big and awkward) is, as he says, derived from 'hulking,' which is a dictionary word. An old dialect glossary confirms this.

Here I would add that in the course of these articles I have had little recourse to dictionaries and glossaries. Instead, I have relied on a random selection from memory. On the other hand, when derivations are questioned, the dictionary often supplies the answer. For instance, the Shorter Oxford English Dictionary tells us that *daddocky*, in common use on the Cotswolds and elsewhere, and meaning 'decayed,' was found in dialect speech as far back as 1624.

It has been pointed out to me that *collogue* is a local variant of 'colloquy,' which in turn is associated with the Latin 'colloquium' and the French 'colloque.' This is true, but I introduced it as a dialect word because in Cotswold speech it carries a shade of meaning implying *confidential* discussion, as distinct from *chunter*, which is associated with amiable gossip.

My same correspondent reminds me of words used in the singular when the plural is involved and instances *sausage* for 'sausages.' I would add that also heard in this way on the Cotswolds are *pound* and *year*. *He was eighty year old*, a native would say; and *I want seven pound of potato.*

An interest in dialect is by no means confined to the male sex, and a lady living in the Vale of Evesham, but with Cotswold associations, includes in her list the following words which I have not previously mentioned:

> *Franz* – for frenzy of raging temper;
>
> *Gleed* – a glowing ember;
>
> *Snigglygog* – a black snail;
>
> *Gaun* – a bowl;
>
> *Ladle-gaun* – a bowl with a long handle for ladling pig-swill;
>
> *Lammeter* – a lame person

BROADWAY, WORCESTERSHIRE.

Then along comes my North Cotswold villager again with, *My 'ooman has got a most izid cold, and her 'a bin a-coughing and ecketting all night long. Izid* is not easy to define; but the speaker meant that his wife had a proper bad cold, just as in another context he would say, *He's a izid good fellow. Ecketting* is completely onomatopoeic and is one of those interesting 'sound pictures' which form an important feature of dialect speech.

While I claim no qualification as a philologist, I can say with confidence that I am Cotswold born and bred. Apparently this is important in village circles. In a Cotswold community some years ago the discussion at the annual parish meeting took a sudden lively turn. One participant in the debate declared, "Mr. Chairman, I ought to know. I've lived in the village for 36 years." An ancient at the back of the room retorted in a stentorian voice which belied his years, *Shut thee rattle! You'm only an evacuee!*

Old Cotswold Dialect: Names of places (29th April 1960)

Many a Cotswold place name is pronounced by the elderly native differently from the spelling on the signpost. In most cases, however, the departure represents an abbreviation. Thus we hear *Stanny* for 'Stanway'; *Broddy* for 'Broadway'; *Cheduth* and *Yanuth* for 'Chedworth' and 'Yanworth'; *Mawsbry* for 'Maugersbury'; *Clapn* for 'Clapton-on-the-Hill'; *Shozzle* for 'Shawswell'; and infrequently *Snozzle* for 'Snowshill.'

A common feature in dialect speech on the Cotswolds and elsewhere is the omission of the initial *w*, such as *'ooman* for 'woman.' There are several 'Woodmancotes' in Gloucestershire, and when I lived in the South Cotswolds, the village that name near Cirencester was referred to by the older folks as *Oodmuckut.*

Some native pronunciations are, however, not abbreviations but noticeable departures from the standard spelling. *Ciceter* for 'Cirencester' is an example of this, but a better one is *Yubberton* compared with 'Ebrington' on the signpost. Chipping Campden has a local pronunciation of its own not easy to spell phonetically – the nearest I can get to it is *Kyandin.'*

All sorts of queer variants arise when the local Cotswold humorist gets to work, whether the subject be place names, house names or field names.

Towards the end of the last century the smallholdings and allotments movement gave the village working man a plot of land that he could cultivate as his own. The fields so let out attracted such names as "Klondike," "Eldorado," "Van Diemen's Land," and "California."

The "California" that I know, consisting of a large field divided into numerous stripes, was quickly abbreviated to "Cali," and for years it was spelt in the rate book that way until an educated assistant overseer came along and changed it to "Calais," which bore no relation to its original appellation.

Unfortunately, some of the fields let out to the farm workers and other villagers were situated on heavy intractable land and once again the local humorist dealt with the situation. "Shepherd's Piece" became "Botany Bay," and another field was quaintly but very appropriately called "Tiresome."

The best example of this local nomenclature that I remember comes from that famous Chipping Campden character, the one and only Ninety Griffin, who during his life as a versatile farm worker did anything on the land from driving a plough to bird-minding in the cherry orchards, and contrived also to serve as a member of the Campden Volunteer Fire Brigade. From time to time Ninety was called upon by his employer to plough a field which bore the delightful name of "Marigold Close." But did Ninety call it "Marigold Close"? Of course not. he said to the lad assigned to lead the horses, *Jump to it, me bwoy! We got to go and plough 'Sally-go-Mad.'*

Christian names are also affected by the local dialect, though nothing like so much as formerly; in fact. *Jarge* for 'George' is now almost confined to stage and radio. But on the Cotswolds in years gone by *Jumps* was a common pronunciation for 'James.' 'Richard' became *Urchard*; 'Elisha' became *Lish*; 'Charles' became *Charl*, or to be more precise, *Charr-ull*; while 'William' was *Willum*, or sometimes all three syllables were separately pronounced *Will-i-um*. For no logical reason 'Alfred' was turned into *Alferd*. *Herbutt* for 'Herbert' is common not only on the Cotswolds but over a much wider area. The most extraordinary departure from the standard christian name that I can think of is *Yudduth* for 'Edward.'

Now for my final story, which can be safely told after the passing of many years since the incident occurred. Country voices can rarely be disguised and when a Cotswold man spoke anonymously in a radio programme he was immediately recognised by listeners in the community in which he lived. He said little that could be questioned until the mentioned that of the licensees of the five public houses in the large village in which he lived, he could only regard one as a truly honest man. That is where the story really beings. One by one, four of the publicans came to him and congratulated him on his outspoken comment. But the fifth licensee had never spoken to the broadcaster from that day to his. He was "the truly honest man." It makes you think!

The Old Cotswold Dialect: A few more words (29th July 1960)

While correspondence reaching me sometimes refers to Cotswold sayings, most inquiries and references relate to individual words which have not appeared in previous articles. Many of these words are associated with the land, such as *hoove* for 'hoe' which is in very common use, as is *waywind* for that obstinate weed, the 'bind-weed,' whose roots seem to go down to Australia. *Pick-thank* for a short hooked stick or a stick with a strong wire attached and used with a bagging hook is now rarely heard, and *dodder*, applied to something in a clover crop, I did not know until a correspondent referred to it. He himself is not certain of its meaning.

The number of words mentioned to me which I have not heard in the North or South Cotswolds is small; but a lady who is a native Chipping Campden and now lives elsewhere asks if I can give her the meaning or origin of *sesserary*. I am unable to do so; but perhaps some Cotswold reader can enlighten us. No doubt it would help if I were to give the context in which the word was used, and I cannot do better than quote my correspondent. "When we were young my father used to give us a word of warning when my mother was inclined to be irritable. He'd say, *Don't get under your mother's feet his morning: she's in a regular sesserary.*"

The lady's reference to her place of birth reminds me that only elderly Cotswold folk now use the word 'native' as a noun when mentioning the place where they were born, e.g. *Stow was my native.*

Other words not quoted previously are: *peart* (lively) and the expression *market-peart* to indicate the state of a farmer who comes home after taking a little extra refreshment with his friends; *trapse* (tramp about) can indicate an unnecessary or tedious journey such as *I trapsed there and back for nothing*; but is more frequently used in the following way: *Don't you go trapsing over my clean floor with your gret fit and them dirty boots.*

Unbeknownst instead of 'unknown' is still heard, as is *unafeared* for 'unafraid,' and less frequently the facetious *underconstumble* for 'understand.'

Teart for 'sore' and *scrump* for 'eat with relish' are fairly common. On the other hand, rarely heard is the attractive *nuzzle* as an alternative to 'nestle.'

Wopse is used by village folk as often as 'wasp'; but *miffy* for 'offended' is infrequent. Some years ago I heard a village child in the Vale of Evesham say of her sister, *Our Mary keeps on flummoxing about. Her flops yur and flops thur and wunt kip still for two minutes.* This restlessness would be described on the Cotswolds as *bumbustling.*

I've noticed over the years that the Cotswold countryman deliberately chooses the pronoun *thee* as a contemptuous substitute for the orthodox 'you.' Thus we hard, *I'm fed up of thee!* and *There's reason in everything; but there's no reason in thee!* I also recall a villager at Honeybourne whose favourite song in demand at informal social gathering is one which consists of a bitter complaint of the intrusion of a lodger into the matrimonial home, each verse concluding with the declaration, *We've got no room for thee!*

I now come to my concluding story. An eccentric villager drowned himself in the millpond, and the usual inquest followed. When announcing their verdict the foreman of the jury added a rider of his own. He said to the coroner, *Suicide while tempry insane*, and continued, *and if I may say, sir, having knowed him this forty years, he was allus tempry insane.*

The Old Cotswold Dialect: More quaint sayings (15th July 1960)

Recent articles have brought me letters adding to my list of topsy-turvy expressions and quaint sayings in local speech. A lad said to father, *Dad, all these blackberries be red.* Whereupon his parent replied, *Of course, you young fool; they be allus red when they be green.*

A farmer correspondent sends me a number of sayings that he has heard from workmen over the years, examples being: *as hollow as a puck-fice* (puff-ball); *as slick as 'oonts* (moles); *as yellow as saffron*; and *as grey as a badger.* This last is heard far beyond the Cotswolds.

By the way, I remember a man with iron-grey hair being described on the North Cotswolds as *mouldy on top.* Another simile rarely heard today is *as lousy as a cuckoo.*

My farmer friend tells me that a native of Temple Guiting who worked for his father used the expression *as fierce as Cox's pig.* In his recollection nobody else ever used it. Is the saying, therefore, exclusive to Temple Guiting? If so, who was Mr. Cox? And finally, in what way did his pig display its aggressive tendencies?

In an earlier contribution I dealt with dialect names for birds, beasts and flowers, and now I'm reminded of *veldver* or *felt* for fieldfare; *mummyruffin* for the long-tailed tit; and *harvest roe* for that attractive little creature, the shrew-mouse. While on the subject, I wonder why, in the South Cotswolds, we used to refer to *Charlie Wagtail*.

My correspondent also remembers a villager who called his light shoes, which he only wore on Sundays and special occasions, his *tea-drinkers*. Years ago when strong boots were the universal wear of farm workers, both on and off duty, a working man who sported shoes was looked upon in the village as a dandy, if not effeminate, and such articles were rather contemptuously referred to not just as 'shoes' but *low-shoes*. Hence the following conversation:

> *From what I've sin of him, that young Joe Brown 'ent overfond of work, master. – What do you expect, missus, with allus wearing them low shoes?*

A middle-aged or elderly woman who wore clothes too young for her age was said to be *dressed up like an old yow* (ewe). When very short dresses and skirts became fashionable for a spell after the First World War a woman said to her neighbour's daughter, *My word, Mary, that's a nice new dress you're wearing.* To which Mary replied, *Oh, it's not new. It's one of Mummy's lengthened.*

Elderly countrymen's similes and metaphors are invariably graphic because they draw spontaneously on their native vocabulary. Some years ago, the village garage proprietor and I had our heads together under the bonnet of my car with an elderly villager as an onlooker who said seriously:

> *More trouble with the car, sir? If you axes me, running a motor is wuss than paying for a love-child. With the one you do know when you've finished paying; but with the tother your hands never out of your pocket.*

Old Cotswold Dialect: More reflections (13th May 1960)

Apart from hearing the native speech of districts other than the Cotswolds, from time to time I have looked at glossaries and studies of dialect in various part of the country and I have reached the conclusion that the Cotswold speech is not only as pleasing to the ear as any of them but as easy for a stranger to follow as any dialect found elsewhere, although, of course, the meanings of some of the truly local words are incomprehensible to a visitor unless explained by their context.

I recently realised something else. Some of our dialect and colloquial words which might be thought to represent modern slang are, in fact, quite old.

Booze, for instance, was in use in connection with drink and drinking before Chaucer's day. *Swop* was employed in a literary sense in the seventeenth century. For instance, John Dryden wrote: "I would have swopped Youth for old age." The Cotswold variants of *drownded* for 'drowned' and *scholard* for 'scholar' can be found in writings of the seventeenth century.

THE FOURTEENTH CENTURY GREVEL'S HOUSE, CHIPPING CAMPDEN.

Since I began writing this series I have kept a sharp look-out for dialect words and phrases that might be new to me or temporarily forgotten because I have not heard them for many years past. In addition, friends and correspondents have given me reminders, with the result that I have acquired what might be called a "supplementary list" for my dialect vocabulary.

Recent reminders include that quaint expression *in co*, broadly meaning 'association with' – perhaps 'in partnership'; but sometimes implying something derogatory such as: *He's done no good to hisself since he got in co with that family.*

Another expression heard less often than formerly is *up the steps*, which is applied to the Police Courts in several Cotswold towns where the magistrates meet on the first floor of the court building. To my mind, one police court at least has lost much of its humour and local character since it was moved from *up the steps* to a modern building where everything is 'on the level.'

Only the other day I heard a woman refer, within the same hour, to:

> *Dunchies* – dumplings in a stew;
>
> *Chibble* (sometimes it's *chobble*) – referring to a child nibbling at an apple; and
>
> *Scrat* – to work hard for a poor living, but also applied to someone who is mean and hard: *Her's too busy a-scratting arter the ha-pence.*

To *feature*, which I heard at the same time, is an old literary word. It means to resemble in facial appearance such as *That child features his grandad.* But why *broccolo* instead of 'broccoli'?

There came a reminder of my boyhood days in the South Cotswolds in *backfriend* – loose skin at the bottom of the finger-nail. On the way out is *cratch* for the tailboard of the carrier's cart, because there are no longer any carriers' carts; just as the *cratch* suspended from the kitchen ceiling is disappearing because there are no longer flitches from the cottage pig to fill it.

Frail for the workman's satchel made of rushes is now rarely heard and hardly ever seen. Yet most country workmen carried them fifty years ago and an aged countryman once told me that he used to go to the river and gather the rushes later to make the *frails* to sell at only threepence each. Closely resembling the *frail* was the old rush *fish-flask.*

When I was a boy, litters of tame rabbits used to get the *tot* – grossly distended stomachs, which often proved fatal, through over-eating greenstuff. Nowadays, few boys keep rabbits and if they do, they are pedigree stock fed on balanced rations which avoid all risk of the *tot.*

My North Cotswold villager has sent me some more dialect words and phrases which he has heard recently, but they must wait until my next contribution, leaving the space in this article to be filled by a Cotswold story. I have culled it from that little masterpiece, "Roger Plowman's Excursion to London". On this occasion, Roger describes in unconscious rustic humour how he tried for the Scripture prize at the village school. For the sake of easy reading, I have simplified the original spelling:

> "Parson come into the school one day, and he had a fire-new book under his arm and said that he should give a prize to the best boy as wrote the most correct account of anything that was in the Bible, and that we were not to have any book to look through. He sat down and said as he should give us half an hour. I'd read about Jezeble over and over again, and knowed it by heart, so I was pretty sure of have the prize. I wrote:
>
> > 'And it come to ass as Jehu rode into Jezreel, he saw Jezeble looking through the winder, and he hollered out to the uniks

that were in the house: 'Throw her out of the winder into the street!' And they throwed her out. And he said, 'Do it the second time.' And they done it the second time. And he said, 'Do it the third time.' And they done it the third time. And he said, 'Do it unto seven times.' And they done it unto seventy times seven. And last of all the 'ooman died also, and they took up of the fragments that were left, ten baskets full.'

"Parson said I'd done fairish well, but there were one or two things not right, and he gied the prize to Sammy Hobbs."

The Old Cotswold Dialect: More words and phrases (27th May 1960)

When I mention *rough music* I'm not referring to the village bandmaster trying out new recruits. I'm thinking of another kind of village band that has for its instruments buckets, trays, tin baths, pots and pans which are beaten with sticks and large spoons to make an unearthly din while the musicians parade outside the home of someone whose behaviour has offended the community.

The custom is one that goes back hundreds of years, but it is over thirty years ago since I last came across it. In my experience as a Cotswolder, rough music falls under three heads. First there's the original and primitive idea of serenading the offender, then there's a display animated by a distorted sense of fun. I recollect this happening when a Cotswold villager 90 years of age took unto himself his third wife. Finally, there's the rough music which takes the form of 'drumming out' an unpopular person or family upon their leaving the village. This is called *ran-tanning*.

I am still being reminded by friends and correspondents of Cotswold words and expressions which have not yet appeared in this series. Such omissions are inevitable; but here are a few not previously mentioned, and again I must point out that some of them are not exclusive to the Cotswolds. In that category comes *Head Sir Rag*, which is used in an ironical way to describe a petty or self-appointed leader. When I mentioned it in a broadcast some years ago a correspondent from Eire suggested that 'Sir Rag' was derived from 'serang' – a Lascar bo'sun.

Free gracious for 'free and gratis' has been mentioned to me. It is heard not only on the Cotswolds but over a much wider area.

Weepy describes a moist soil or a cut or wound that is discharging.

Empt for the verb 'to empty,' and *burrow* for 'sheltered' are very common; but heard less frequently is *watty-handed* for a 'left-handed' person.

Loose is employed for 'release' or 'let out,' as in the case of a Cotswold farmer's warning to some officials whom he found on his land without their giving prior notice: *If you 'ent off these premises within five minutes, I shall loose the bull!*

Jack-up is infrequently heard. It means 'to throw up' or 'relinquish,' such as *jack-up a job*, or, among children, to *jack-up* a game that they are playing.

While *warnuts* is a common pronunciation of 'walnuts,' *wetchered* for getting 'wet-through' is almost a by-gone.

I came across recently, in an account of country life in the mid-19th century, a reference to *tay-kettle broth*, which I had not heard since a boy. As I remember it, when used as a substitute for tea which was very expensive in those days, it consisted of toast soaked in hot water to give it colour; or as a weak soup it was made in the same way but with a few onions added and pepper and salt introduced to improve its taste. These are my recollections of the meanings of the expression, and I stand to be corrected by someone with a longer memory than mine.

Tempest is still used by elderly countryfolk in relation to a threatened thunderstorm. They look at the heavy sky and say, *I reckon we'm going to have a tempest.*

The cottage pig has virtually disappeared with the old village pig clubs wound up, and it was pleasing to read in these columns recently Mr. A.R. Butler's graphic account of the ritual of pig-killing half a century ago. It reminded me of *scrattings* – the crisp bits left after the leaf had been rendered down for lard. My Devonshire-born grandmother called them *crittens* or *crittings*. At the same time I am reminded of a conversation between two elderly villagers which I overheard a few years ago.

> Harry said to Alfred, *I don't think I shall have me another pig. I reckon the bacon from the last 'un cost me well-nigh five bob a pound.*
>
> Some ten seconds' silence followed, and Alfred replied: *Maybe: but I likes me a nice rasher of home-cured on me plate of a morning. Why some o' this boughten tackle must 'a bin dipped – not cured.*
>
> He puffed at his pipe thoughtfully, then added, as an unconscious illustration of practical economics, *I must allow that feeding a pig nowadays costs a mort of money, Harry; but I allus arges: you can count pound notes, but you can't yut 'em.*

And so say all of us, including the Aberdonian who wrote to his local newspaper recently asking what the *old* pound note looked like.

The Old Cotswold Dialect: Some more old words and phrases (17th June 1960)

Still more old Cotswold words spring to the memory when I thought that my stock of them had been exhausted. Mr. H. Raymond Smith referred recently in the correspondence columns to *wacky-handed* compared with my *watty-handed* and said that he heard it as a schoolboy on the cricket field. My pronunciation of it came from the South Cotswolds where I used to hear in cricket parlance the word *cut* meaning a scoring stroke. For instance, a member of the team would say, *We shouldn't have made much of a score if old Harry Higgins hadn't cut a fyow fowers and sixes.*

Hit for a good crop, especially of fruit, is less frequently heard than formerly, as is *lother* for 'ladder.'

Outride for traveller seems to have died out. Perhaps it went when the representative of the local tradesman or country brewery ceased ot use a pony and trap to do his rounds. A few travellers made their journeys on horseback, and in some instances relied upon a knowing and sober nag to deliver them safely home!

Some of the old words however, died hard. I asked a Cotswold farmer how his father was and received the reply, *Not so bad for an old 'un; he keeps on puddling about*, meaning that he continued to potter around the farm in leisurely fashion.

Middling is an unusual word, for it has two separate meanings. Normally it implies a *fair* state of affairs: but when preceded by 'very' or 'proper' and applied to a person's health it indicates a serious situation; in fact, if I'm told that an elderly person is *proper middling* he may well be on his last legs. It's equivalent to the hospital notice, "Very poorly."

When I was a boy it was not uncommon for a greenhorn to be sent to the farm for some *pigeon's milk*, and there were facetious references to a *mare's egg* – presumably laid in a mare's nest!

I heard years ago of two townsmen visiting a Cotswold village who saw an allotment holder awkwardly carrying an outsize pumpkin. When asked what it was, he replied. *This yur be a mare's egg.* Old Bill told the story later in the village inn and declared that he had sold it for a shilling to "two London cockneys." Why <u>London</u> cockneys? The last time I heard the expression it came from Harry Baker of Yubberton.

Unusually in modern literature and conversation *wench* has a derogatory meaning; but not among the older Cotswold folk. Nor did Shakespeare use it in reproachful sense. On the contrary, a previous village generation might even use it as an indication of affection. *Come and help me peel these taters, my good wench*, a mother would say, meaning 'my good girl.'

Set is a word that has a variety of meanings. It is employed instead of 'let,' as in *I hear old Dan'l Brown has set his farm*. It is commonly heard in place of 'sat,' e.g. *He set himself down in that very chair*. Yet another alternative relates to planting. Runner beans or potatoes are *set* with a dibber, as distinct from peas, which may be sown or drilled. This reminds me that I found the following couplet in a little book printed nearly 300 years ago: *In gardening, ne'er this rule forget. Sow dry; set wet*. Generally speaking, the precept still holds good.

Chimney for what is known nowadays as a 'fireplace' was once in common use on the Cotswolds, although I would say that the term ought to be confined to the open fireplace and inglenook where one can bend down, look up and see the sky. An occasional variant for 'chimney' was *chimmuck*.

MICKLETON, GLOS.

Many years ago during alterations to a village inn well known in the Four Shires a splendid open fireplace in Cotswold stone was uncovered behind former plaster. Visitors to the inn greatly admired it, and it attracted the attention of an artist who came down from London specially to paint it. The landlady (who told me the story) was naturally proud of this, and when an elderly customer came in for his evening cup of cider, she said to him. *D'you know, William, we've had a famous artist down from London to paint that chimney*. Always polite, William immediately replied, *Well, I must say ma'am, it look all the better for it*.

The Old Cotswold Dialect: Unconscious humour (1ˢᵗ July 1960)

The unconscious humour which prompts the remark, "That sounds Irish to me," is by no means confined to the Emerald Isle, and I received recently from a Shipston-on-Stour octogenarian some examples in the Cotswold dialect. He remembers the following sayings of an old roadman:

All my bet taters be bad.

Yur! Put this bit o' string in your pocket; then you'll have some when you've got none.

I tied my hoss to a gap in the hedge, and when I got back he were gone.

Mention of string reminds me of the injunction given to me as a schoolboy: *Always have shilling, a knife, and a bit of string in your pocket.*

A generation ago there was a character in most districts noted for these queer sayings. Until the First World War, the aristocrat of potatoes was the Black Kidney, which prompted a man to declare: *You ought to see my Black Kidneys: when they be boiled they be as yaller as snowballs.*

Another character was eating jam sandwiches for his lunch while all his mates had meat in theirs. He dolefully remarked, *These yur'd be capital biff samwiches if only the missus had had some mate to put in 'em* (note the pronunciation – *samwiches*).

This topsy-turvy talk is found in almost every complete Mummers' Play which represents the oldest form of peasant humour. In the middle of the play, a character (usually Doctor Finney) reels off at speed a succession of nonsensical phrases such as:

I went a little further and I met a mon on hoss-back underneath a mare's belly with a glow-worm stuck in his tail to light him the road... I knocked at the maid and out come the door... We got one of the funniest sights theest ever did see down in our back cellar. It's a little kid stripped naked with all his clothes on.

By the way, I referred to an earlier article to *lew-warm* for 'luke-warm' and now I am reminded of *star-naked* for 'stark-naked.'

A natural home for these quaint expressions is, of course, Yubberton. A rhyme that the late Sam Bennett, of Ilmington, used to recite was:

Old Sam Keyte, as I've heard say,
Kill a cock because he wouldn't lay.

I recall several country workers who used to speak in rough and ready rhyme, especially when *chuntering* with cronies at the village inn. Their doggerel was usually delivered in couplets, such as: *I've worked eight hours this day, and I think I've earned my pay.* Or: *I said when I sin the sun a-setting, 'tis stormy weather we'll be getting.* This was accepted by the company as normal conversation and a stranger who laughed at it was soon rebuked.

There are many amusing stories about farm workers who were sacked or threatened with dismissal; but here is an account of a very old servant who wished to seek pastures new.

Old George went to the farmer who employed him and announced, without notice, *Master, I wants to gen 'ee a wick's notice.* The farmer was completely taken aback. "Whatever are you talking about, George? Why, you must have been with me and my old dad nigh on fifty years." *That's sure to be right, master, forty-nine year come Michaelmas.* Then George added thoughtfully, *And that's just what's a-worritting me, master. I reckons that if I gus on as I'm a-guing I shall get meself into a rut.* The farmer laughed. "You know the old motto, George – a rolling stone gathers no moss." *And a gate-post no knowledge, nor a setting hen no fathers*, George promptly retorted. But they settled it in the end. George agreed to stay on *another five year – just tempry.*

The Old Cotswold Dialect: Reader's Answers (12th August 1960)

In my last article I made inquiry as to the meaning or origin of two words, in the hope that readers would supply the answers. The first reply came by telephone a few hours after the "Journal" was out. It related to *dodder* and the reader informed me that it was a parasitic plant well known to farmers. If I wished, he would supply me with its Latin name. I thanked him for kindly giving me the information so promptly. Then I thought, "Can it be a dictionary word and not dialect, as my original correspondent imagined?" I found the word mentioned in three dictionaries, with Chambers' definition as follows: "dodder (n), a leafless, twining, pale parasitic plant (Cuscuta) of or akin to the convolvulus family."

The other word I inquired about was *sesserary*, and a genial correspondent calling himself a "Campden Old 'Un" tells me: "This was a very common expression years ago and was always used when referring to someone who was in a very bad temper, but more so of a woman than a man. You would hear someone say: *What's the matter of old Mrs. So-and-So? Her yunt half in a sesserary.*"

Another reader from Warwickshire states that her mother, who is 85 years of age, uses the word regularly. She adds that her mother also refers to a very sharp frost as a *remur*. This is, I think, the sam word as that used in various circumstances on the Cotswolds to denote something sharp or strong. For instance, it used to be employed in village cricket circles to indicate a forcing stroke by a batsman, such as *Old Harry won us the match when he cut a proper reamer off their fast bowler*. This same old lady says to a visitor who calls on her dressed up and smart, *My word, aren't you nobby?*

Several correspondents send me words such as *yup* for 'heap' and *yud-fust* for 'head-first.' They are, of course, local pronunciations of standard words; but nevertheless interesting as an important element of Cotswold speech. In passing, I would mention a common mispronunciation in the South and North Cotswolds and probably elsewhere. That is *refuge* for 'refuse' as applied to rubbish, e.g. *I sin the council refuge lorry in the village this morning, so I put my bin out.*

Reeved is another word which I have not previously listed. It means 'wrinkled' or 'puckered.' For instance, a girl would say to her companion, *D'you know the back of your dress is all reeved up?* Or a mother would reprove her daughter, *Don't reeve up your forehead like that when you're reading.*

A regular correspondent from Shipston-on-Stour draws my attention to the wide range of interesting nicknames used in earlier days in villages and small towns; but that is a subject which needs careful handling, especially as some of the soubriquets were far from complimentary! If dealt with at all, the subject must be deferred until a later contribution.

My concluding story is a reminder that the ostensibly slow-thinking villager is sometimes possessed of a gift for sharp repartee. Some Birmingham visitors called at an old inn well known in the Four Shires which, at the time, held a beer and wine licence only. A lady inquired rather querulously of the son of the house, "But haven't you any spirits?" *No; I'm sorry, mam*, came the instant answer, *but we've got a smartish few ghosts*. And so they had! The several local apparitions differed in form; but they had one common characteristic – they always walked soon after 10pm.

The Old Cotswold Dialect: A private collection (28ᵗʰ August 1960)

Knowing my interest in the subject, a North Cotswold villager has sent me from time to time over the year local words and expressions used by himself or heard in conversation. He has compiled his own glossary in alphabetical order and it contains several hundred words and phrases. It is different from other glossaries, however, because the words are listed without any definitions, for the simple reason that our village lexicographer knows all the answers! As I already had a written or mental note of them, many of the words have been included in earlier articles; but other have not been previously quoted. I therefore propose to mention some of them in this and the next instalment.

Beginning alphabetically, I notice *abide* for 'bear,' e.g. *I can't abide that 'ooman's tongue.* Then we see *afeared* for 'afraid' and *astart* for 'startled.'

Boffle has a meaning somewhat different from 'baffle' from which it is derived. Instead of the standard definition of "to puzzle and bewilder" it implies distraction of interference with one's concentration. A dart-thrower taking aim amid joking remarks addressed to him by onlookers would exclaim: *Shut thee rattle. You'm only trying to boffle me.*

Butty is shown as a workmate or a companion. It is in common use as such on the Cotswolds and also elsewhere.

Cherricuds is largely confined to speech on the farm, for it means the first milking after calving.

Cratch I have mentioned previously as applied to the tail-board of a wagon (particularly the old carrier's cart) and the slatted container suspended from the kitchen ceiling to hold bacon. My friend's glossary reminds me that is it also used in connection with the wooden frame which holds fodder for cattle in the fields or yards.

Cother means to gather together in whispered conference. An old man would say to his companion in the village inn, *I warn they be up to summat, a-cothering over there in the corner.*

Dillen is the weakling of the litter; *faddle* means to finick; and *glurr* is to slide on ice. The use of the two *r*'s in this last word reminds me that my North Cotswold friend has his own method of phonetic spelling which is very effective, for *glurr* is pronounced with an accentuated *r* very much as a Scot would speak it.

Ettle is an abbreviation of 'nettle' in the same way as *ginsurd* is a shortened pronunciation of 'greensward.'

A *jibber* is a horse that won't pull, while a *ligger* is a liar.

A *maiding-tub* (sometimes called a 'dolly-tub') used to be applied to a large deep tub in which the dirty clothes were placed. In those days the 'washing machine' was a woman with strong arms.

Now for a few old Cotswold phrases. Among the oldsters one can still hear, *He won't be said,* instead of "He won't be gainsaid."

A *wooden 'ooman* is a breast plough, which was used for skimming, especially on smallholdings and allotments.

Some years ago I saw a man working with a breast plough on an allotment at Yubberton and I realised what an effective implement it could be in skilled hands. My companion was a Yubbertonian and he said innocently, *That's funny.* I asked, "What's funny?" He replied, *He 'ant got a bucket of water of him.* "Why on earth should he want that?" This brought the solemn reply, *Oh, he most generally gets the blade red hot.* Well may the natives declare that Yubberton is the places where all the fools *come to!*

In a form, meaning to an exceptional degree or in emphatic manner, is still in common use, e.g. *The gaffer was proper upset and he cussed him in a form.*

The old-fashioned country worker usually has the most ready and ingenious excuses when rebuked or reproved. There was one such man on the Cotswolds who was often in trouble for being late though lived only a stone's throw away from his place of employment. The farmer said to him, "How is it that you're always a few minutes late, Tom, when you live just across the way? Yet Harry, here, who has six miles to bike, is always on time or early." Tom answered instantly, *It's easy for Harry, master. He lives so far away, if he starts late he got time to ketch up.*

The Old Cotswold Dialect: More from a private collection (9th September 1960)

Here is a further selection from the privately compiled glossary of a North Cotswold villager mentioned in my last article.

Dabster for 'expert' is in common use and so is *dabhand*. Less frequently heard are *eaning* (lambing) and *draggle-tail* (a slattern). In both the North and South Cotswolds, potato haulms are referred to as *hams*.

I observe that my friend's list includes *dancing-ducks*, which I am told means peas roasted on a shovel; but I doubt whether the expression has any special Cotswold associations.

Graft has nothing to do with bribery, but relates to hard work, such as, *When I took on that job o' digging I didn't count on it being such hard graft.*

Eyeable for 'presentable' is an attractive dialect alternative, while *mewl* for 'cry' is onomatopoeic.

Pitchipoll not only means to turn a somersault; it is used in connection with the turning over of an investment profitably, generally on a basis of 100 per cent. For example, *I paid a smartish price for that orchard of cider fruit; but it done me well. It pitchipolled the first season.*

Proud-bellied is a down-to-earth way of saying that a man is conceited.

Others in the list include *nub* (to shine); *piddling* (trifling); *rocksy* (over-ripe) and akin to *mawsy*.

Then I come to *sad* meaning 'heavy' and sometimes applied to food that has been overcooked. This brings me to a letter which I recently received from a gentleman who lived in Chipping Campden for many years. A long time ago, he asked a Campden workman who was doing some land-draining how it was going, and the man replied that it was a *sadden job*. When asked the meaning of the word, the native said it meant hard digging and was always used by the old men engaged in such work. He did not know the spelling of the word.

Now for some more individual words. *Slammerkin* is a 'slut' or 'trollop,' *slams* stands for 'sloes,' and *sidlip* for the vessel that was used to carry the seed corn when sowing was down by hand, *broadcasting* – a job that called for considerable skill to ensure the even distribution of the grain over the field.

Sned or *snead* is a scythe handle; *tallet* a loft; and to turn to something quite different – *geeohing* means driving the plough with two horses abreast. The word is used far beyond the Cotswolds.

My eye caught a most extraordinary expression – *nursing the iron baby*. It was explained to me that, many years ago, prisoners in certain jails in this country were made ot hold up a heavy weight in each hand for long periods. It was probably the successor to the treadmill and was known among the men as "nursing the iron baby." The glossary certainly does not lack variety!

Other expressions recorded are: *He's sure to go to jebbardy* (jeopardy); *He's a bit finicky over his fettle* meaning 'He's fussy over his food.'

Didn't that forever rain indicates something different from *dabbly* which relates to a showery spell of weather.

I must not forget my story. A reported had called upon a Cotswold couple who were celebrating their diamond wedding. Old George was seated comfortably in an armchair at the fireside, smoking a cigar which had been given to him, while his wife was seen to be preparing a meal through the open door leading into the kitchen. The reporter said to George, who was a retired farm worker, "They tell me, Mr. Smith, that you brought up your large family on eleven shillings a week." Old George raised a warning finger, *Shssh! Not so loud, if you please, I allus told the missus I only got ten!*

The Old Cotswold Dialect: Summing up, and the outlook for the future (30th September 1960)

What have we learned from our examination of the varied aspects of the old Cotswold dialect? First, I think, that although it may be declining and a degree of standardisation in local pronunciation is taking place, it is by no means dead. Furthermore, the use of dialect is not confined to the older generation, although in general the elderly make more use of it than the young people of the region.

It is obvious, also, that dialect produces words and expressions with colour and shades of meaning often absent from or unattainable in standard English. Because of this, a Cotswold native is rarely inarticulate in what may be called his 'mother tongue.' Interesting proof of this is revealed in the story of the North Cotswold farm worker who was the only witness of the capers of a motorist who eventually landed in a ditch. He was suspected of "driving under the influence" and the local policeman interviewed old Sam, who insisted that the motorist was not drunk, then added a solemn rider, *But I must allow that he'd had the best part of a smartish fyow* (few). The policeman knew what Sam meant – the motorist was in that intermediate state between drunkenness and sobriety. I suggest, however, that the dialect description represents a nice distinction which could hardly have been attained in standard English.

In John Darke's "Sojourn on the Cotswolds" (published in 1890) the author remarks on the habit of his host (a Cotswold farmer) of "uttering sentences which had the metrical rhythmical flow of blank verse." Without doubt, this unconscious rhythm has survived.

Another conclusion reached is that a sharp difference exists between the loose or general term – "dialect" – and the genuine article. I have always been firmly of the opinion that nobody can speak the authentic dialect of a particular locality unless he has heard it and learnt it either as a native or during the young formative years. We have seen grow up since the introduction of radio a synthetic form of dialect known in the BBC as "Loamshire" which cannot be assigned to any particular country of district and which is sometimes called "Cornish Cockney." Many occasions and settings arise in radio and television drama and features where it is expressly intended not to identify the locality of the play. On the other hand, it is essential to indicate a rural background. The use of "Loamshire" in such circumstances is justified.

What annoys the native is a spurious imitation of his local speech, and just as it is said the camera cannot lie, nor can the microphone. The incompetent imitation is spotted immediately. I like the story of the music hall comedian who was showing off his Scots accent and speech in the lounge of a northern hotel after hours. Following a few anecdotes he asked his audience, "Now who can tell me what part of Scotland I come from?" A dour old man who had been sitting quietly in a corner snapped, "Penzance!"

I call to mind listening to an Upper Slocombe comedy of mine being broadcast. Much of it was in the Cotswold dialect. An actor of national repute in relation to dialects had been included in the cast. From a dramatic point of view his performance was faultless but he was hopelessly out of touch alongside the Cotswold natives with their authentic voices. I realised once again that there can be few dialects more difficult to imitate than Cotswold.

It has its equal in this respect, however, in the dialect of old Evesham, particularly Bengeworth. This was confirmed when I listened to "The Journal" dialect correspondent Ben Judd give an illustrated talk on the subject. Although I have resided in the Vale of Evesham for over 30 years, I've never attempted to imitate the local dialect, and listening to Ben Judd showed me how wise I was.

Before we approach the final question: "Will the old Cotswold dialect survive?" there is a prior query to be disposed of, and that is: "Is it worth preserving, anyway?" here I recall a Countryman's Conference which I attended some years ago, where a village schoolmaster described dialect as being nothing more than slovenly English. "The sooner it is killed or dies out, the better!" he declared.

He was no doubt thinking of such expressions as *her don't like she*. But probably also in his mind was the handicap of a marked country accent (other than Scots) to someone intent on pursuing an academic or professional career.

It is, of course, a question of degree and the answer is found in the fortunate countryman who is bi-lingual; that is to say, one who can use and understand his native speech and also express himself in academic English without an accent that irritates. A prefect example of this bi-lingual country speaker is F.H. Grisewood, who learnt his dialect as a boy when his father was a parson in a Cotswold village.

There are, of course, countrymen and particularly broadcasters, ranging from A.G. Street and Ralph Wightman to members of "The Archers," whose truly rural voices, like the milkmaid's comely face, represent their fortune.

After that digression, I return to the important question: "Will the Cotswold dialect survive?" I feel confident that it will be with us for a long time yet – in fact so long as countrymen chunter and collogue in the village inn and while angry Cotswold parents chide their youngsters.

A BBC producer now holding a high position in the Corporation used to tell a story of his first assignment as a newcomer to the Midland Region, which took him to Chipping Campden. Unacquainted with the district he wisely wanted to obtain an idea of the local background and particularly the local speech, and he was advised to sit quietly in the bar of a certain inn at Chipping Campden and listen to the natives talking among themselves. The producer introduced himself to the landlord and said, "I'm told that if I sit quietly in here I shall be certain to hear the true rich Cotswold dialect." The landlord was obviously puzzled; so puzzled in fact that he pushed back his hat to scratch his head. *Dialect? Dialect?* he said, *I dunno about that.* Then he added firmly, *We all talks natchrul in yur.*

Whether it is just sentiment or not, so far as I am concerned it will be a sad day when the landlord of the Campden inn and many like it can no longer say:

We all talks natchrul in yur.

Glossary

The glossary below contains occasional references to Shakespeare's plays. The intention here is twofold: first, it makes this glossary look far more learned than it really is, and second, it helps demonstrate that the plays of Shakespeare are, almost certainly, written by a local man (rather than, say, Francis Bacon or the Earl of Oxford). Jesse Salisbury remarked:

> "There is abundant evidence throughout the writings of Shakespeare, that he was well acquainted with this locality and its dialect. Indeed, it would be strange if such were not the case... Stratford is only twelve miles or so from Evesham 'as the crow flies,' and the difference in the dialects of the two districts is slight... It may be urged, that some of these words are mere survivals of the speech of all England, in Shakespeare's day. In certain cases this may be so; but it is scarcely credible that this can apply to many; for it would be hard to supply a valid reason, why a greater number of these (if once generally common) words, should remain current in the neighbourhood of Shakespeare's birth, rather than elsewhere."

A	*Verb*	To have, present and imperative moods: *I bin a-waterin the flowers* and *he was a-going*
A	*Pron*	He; she; it: *Where is a?* (Henry V II.III & III.II)
A	*Prep*	In; on: *Ers a bed uv a bwile a top uv er yud*
Abear	*Verb*	To endure. *I caunt abear the sight o' im*
Above-a-bit	*Adv*	Extremely *(adverbial phrase)*
Afore	*Verb*	Before: *Come an' see uz afore ee gooes away*
Agate	*Verb*	Going on: *What's agate now, you?*
Aim	*Verb*	To attempt. *Er aimed to do it*
Akere	*Verb*	Look here; or, come here
All-as-is	*Phrase*	All that remains

All-is-one	*Phrase*	All the same (Merry Wives of Windsor, II.II)
Along with	*Verb*	With, as in *I left the money along with Mr. Frost*
An-all	*Adv*	Also
Anant	*Prep*	Opposite: *Put em yur anant the door*
Argify	*Verb*	To argue
As like to	*Phrase*	Probable or likely
Assud	*Adj*	Contrary (as in 'Arseward')
Assud-bakkuds	*Adj*	Back to front
Aw-puck	*Noun*	Will-o-the-wisp (also **hobbady-lantern** and **pinket**) (Midsummer Night's Dream)
Back-friend	*Noun*	A secret enemy
Back-side	*Noun*	The back of a house (not to be confused with **assud**).
Badger	*Verb*	To torment
Bag	*Noun*	The udder of a cow, or three bushels of corn
Bag	*Verb*	To cut wheat, barley, &c, with a *bagging-hook* rather than a *sickle*.
Bawk	*Verb*	To hinder
Be-call	*Verb*	To abuse
Belly-full	*Noun*	A sufficient or excessive quantity (Lear III.II)
Better	*Adv*	More: *I bin yur better 'n hour*
Bezzle	*Verb*	To drink immoderately

Bit	*Adj*	A small amount, though also used more generally, as in *a bit of stick* meaning a walking stick.
Bother	*Noun*	Trouble
Brevit	*Verb*	To hunt about; to pry inquisitively: *I've brevitted all over, and I still can't find it.*
Broken-mouthed	*Adj*	Without teeth (All's Well That Ends Well II.III)
Buckle	*Noun*	A tough slip of wood used to fasten thatch to a roof
Buckle	*Verb*	To bend (II Henry IV I.I)
Cadge	*Verb*	To beg (making a beggar a **cadger**)
Cag-mag	*Verb*	To grumble at, or nag.
Cank	*Verb*	To (incessantly) chatter
Casselty	*Adj*	Uncertain: *This be casselty weather*
Chawl	*Verb*	To chew slowly
Chawl	*Verb*	To repeat words which have given offence
Chawl	*Noun*	The lower jaw of a pig
Chock-full	*Adj*	Completely full
Chops	*Noun*	Mouth
Chup	*Adj*	Cheap
Clack	*Verb*	To chatter incessantly; or idle talk
Clout	*Noun*	A rag or cloth (King John III.IV; Richard III I.III; Hamlet II.II)

Clout	*Noun*	An iron plate nailed to an axle to prevent it wearing away
Cokers	*Noun*	Reapers, particularly those who have travelled from far away
Colley	*Noun*	Soot; coal-black; smuttiness
Colley	*Verb*	To blacken
Conker	*Noun*	A snail shell
Consaits	*Verb*	Fancies or imagines
Craichy	*Adj*	Weak; infirm; shaky. *I be a craichy old mon now, you*
Cricket	*Noun*	A little stool
Cunning	*Adj*	Suspiciously clever or talented. A **cunning man** or **woman** might be a witch (2 Henry VI IV.1)
Cuther	*Verb*	To whisper confidentially
Dabbly	*Verb*	Uncertain, especially in connection with weather
Dabster	*Noun*	An expert (also **dab-hand**)
Dadduck	*Noun*	Anything rotten (but especially wood)
Differ	*Verb*	To quarrel
Do-er-mouth	*Verb*	To kiss
Domber	*Verb*	To smoulder
Donny	*Noun*	The hand, especially the hand of child
Dromedary	*Noun*	A dull or stupid person
Dubbid	*Adj*	Blunt

Dummill	*Noun*	A useless article (also **dummuck**)
Edge o'night	*Noun*	At dusk
Ellun	*Noun*	Elder
Elven	*Noun*	Elm
Entany	*Noun*	A narrow passage or by-street. In Pershore, leading out of Bridge Street, there was a narrow passage called 'Bachelor's Entany.'
Fidther	*Verb*	To make a slight rustling sound, like a cat or mouse in straw
Find-liss	*Noun*	A valuable article found by accident
Fire-new	*Adj*	New (Shakespeare, Love's Labour's Lost I.1)
Fittle	*Noun*	Food
Fot	*Verb*	Fetched or brought
Fritch	*Adj*	Conceited or vain
Gaffer	*Noun*	Boss or master.
Gallus	*Adj*	Wicked and impudent, or daring and impertinent (possibly originating as an shortened form of 'gallows fodder') (compare Love's Labour's Lost V.2)
Gammits	*Noun*	Jokes or tricks
Gin	*Verb*	Gave. *I a-gin im a whack on is yud wiv my stick*
Gleed	*Noun*	Red embers of a fire
Go-back	*Verb*	To die

Good	*Adj*	A substantial amount: *a good while* (say, seven or eight months).
Grist	*Noun*	Corn to be ground (applied to small quantities)
Gyawky	*Noun*	An awkward or stupid person
Happen		Perhaps (Hamlet V.II)
Hegler	*Noun*	Itinerant dealer in poultry, eggs, etc.
Hommucks	*Noun*	Feet
Hook	*Noun*	A hook (though the phrase "take thee hook" loosely translates as "go away")
Housen	*Noun*	Houses
Hud	*Noun*	Husk or shell (also called **hulls**)
Hunkid	*Adj*	Very bad or dreadful
Inchmeal	*Adv*	Bit by bit (Tempest II.II)
Innuds	*Noun*	Innards or bowels
Jerkum	*Noun*	Rough plum wine
Job	*Verb*	To stab with a sharp implement
Jommuck	*Verb*	To shake about roughly
Jud	*Verb*	Dead: *'im be judded.* Other phrases for death include **shut-his-knife, stuck-his-spoon-in-the-wall,**
Keffle	*Noun*	Anything of inferior quality
Laggy	*Adj*	Applied to timber with a natural crack inside
Learn	*Verb*	To teach

Lection	*Noun*	Chance or probability
Limmel	*Adv*	Torn to pieces (Cymbeline II.IV)
Lin-pin	*Noun*	Linch-pin
Lollock	*Verb*	Resting in an idle or listless manner
Luny	*Adj*	Imbecile
Lush	*Verb*	To beat (typically with green boughs)
Lush	*Noun*	A green bough (to use for beating)
Mammet	*Noun*	A scarecrow or puppet (Romeo and Juliet III.V)
Mawkin	*Noun*	A scarecrow (Coriolanus II.II; Pericles IV.IV)
Mawkin	*Noun*	A bundle of rags tied to a stick as a make-shift mop
Mawsey	*Adj*	Over-ripe or rotten
Metheglin	*Noun*	Mead (that is, liquor made from honey) (Love's Labour's Lost V.II; Merry Wives of Windsor V.V)
Middling	*Adj*	Unwell or indifferent
Mighty	*Adv*	Very
Mishtiful	*Adj*	Mischievous
Miskin	*Noun*	A dung-heap or refuse heap
Missis	*Noun*	The wife
Mizzle	*Noun*	Slight rain (like drizzle but less serious)
Moithered	*Verb*	To be bothered, dazed or delirious

Momble	*Verb*	To puzzle or bewilder
Mommuck	*Noun*	An untidily or absurdly-dressed person
Morum	*Noun*	A mechanical invention; boyish trick or ingenious idea
Nalls	*Noun*	Belongings
Nation	*Adv*	Very
Nesh	*Adj*	Tender or delicate
Nifle-pin	*Noun*	A pretended occupation, which is really an excuse for being idle.
Noggen	*Adj*	Clumsy or inept.
Noggen	*Noun*	Someone who is clumsy or inept, someone with a wooden head.
Odd	*Adj*	Strange or peculiar (compare As You Like It III)
Ourn	*Pron*	Ours
Out-ride	*Noun*	A commercial traveller
Own to	*Verb*	To admit of confess to
Peart	*Adj*	Bright or lively
Pendle	*Noun*	Clock pendulum
Pharisees	*Noun*	Fairies (rare in the 1890s)
Pick-thank	*Noun*	A censorious person (1 Henry IV III.II)
Pikelet	*Noun*	Crumpet
Pill	*Noun*	A shallow well fed with surface water
Pinkit	*Noun*	Will-o'-th'-wisp

Plim	*Adj*	To swell in cooking (especially applied to bacon)
Plim	*Noun*	A plumb-line
Poking	*Verb*	Gleaning or leazing a field a second time (perhaps because most of the gleanings consist of ears of corn only, which can be put into a pocket).
Porker	*Noun*	A pig suitable for killing for pork
Pot	*Noun*	Container (usually wicker) for fruit or potatoes, commonly holding about five pecks
Purgy	*Adj*	Peevish or short-tempered
Quilt	*Verb*	To beat
Rag-stone	*Noun*	Rough stone used for sharpening scythes &c. (also called a **rubber**)
Random	*Adj*	Wild or prodigal (also used of those **taters** which appear where none have been planted).
Rime	*Noun*	Hoar-frost
Rivel	*Verb*	To shrivel or wrinkle
Ropy	*Adj*	Stringy or poor.
Roxed	*Adj*	(of a pear) ripe and soft; (of a cough) loose and easy
Saded	*Adj*	Tired
Sapy	*Adj*	Moist or soft
Scrat	*Verb*	To scratch; to work hard; to scrape together

Scrogging	*Verb*	Gathering the apples left after the main crop has been gathered
Scud	*Noun*	Slight shower
Shard	*Noun*	A gap or opening in a hedge
Ship	*Noun*	Sheep. The old inspiration behind the names of Shipton and Shipston. (Two Gentleman of Verona I.I; Comedy of Errors IV.I). New Street, Bengeworth, used to be known as "Ship's-yud Row" (Sheep's-head Row), probably after a beer-shop.
Shog-off	*Verb*	Go away (Henry V II.I; Hamlet I.II)
Shog-trot	*Noun*	A steady amble
Shookey	*Noun*	A tea-kettle
Shucks	*Noun*	Husks
Skew-bald	*Adj*	Piebald. 'Th' apparatour upon his skew-bald'd horse' (Cleaveland, 1651)
Skimmington	*Noun*	A procession in which effigies of an objectionable person is carried through the village accompanied by raucous noise, perhaps with odd bits of clothing as banners. If all goes well, the procession culminates with the burning of the effigies.
Skurruck	*Noun*	The smallest part or fraction
Slaith	*Noun*	Action, form or manner of working
Sling	*Noun*	A narrow road or lane (a **slinget** is a narrow strip of ground)
Slinger	*Noun*	A narrow strip of ground
Slipping	*Noun*	A cutting from a plant

Glossary

Slommuck	*Verb*	To shuffle along in an ungainly manner
Slow-swift	*Noun*	One who is slow at work
Smartish	*Adj*	Fairly well or good
Smock-faced	*Adj*	Modest looking
Smudge	*Verb*	To kiss
Sour ground	*Noun*	Unfertile or ill-drained ground
Starky	*Adj*	Dry and hard
Stick-and-rag	*Noun*	An umbrella
Stock	*Verb*	To peck as a bird
Stodgier	*Noun*	A thick or fat one
Stretcher	*Noun*	A story or assertion which stretches belief
Sucked-in	*Verb*	Cheated
Swanky	*Noun*	Very poor beer or cider (if sour it's called **swipes**)
Swyme	*Verb*	To feel giddy
Tabber	*Verb*	To make a drumming noise; to tap with a stick or with the fingers
Tack	*Noun*	Anything of inferior quality; stuff (also an alternative name for Jerkum, for painfully obvious reasons).
Talks	*Verb*	Says
Tang	*Verb*	To call bees, when they are swarming, by making a noise (often with a fire shovel or warming pan and door-key)
Throw-back	*Verb*	To give discount

Throw-back	*Noun*	The discount given
Tiddling	*Noun*	A lamb or other animal brought up by hand
Tidy	*Adj*	Good, fine, sound, in solid health
Tissick	*Verb*	Cough
Tom-and-Jerry	*Noun*	Beer-house
Tom-fool	*Noun*	The fool who accompanies the Morris dancers
Tommy-bag	*Noun*	Bag to carry food in (also called **fittle-bag**)
Tottery	*Adj*	Infirm
Tump	*Noun*	Small hill or hillock (either in the landscape or of **taters**)
Tushes	*Noun*	Tusks
Unbeknowns		Without knowledge: *unbeknowns-to-him the cart 'ad already gone*
Unkid	*Adj*	Lonely
Watty-onded	*Adj*	Left-handed
Wench	*Noun*	A girl (Tempest I.II and II.I; Two Gentlemen of Verona II.VII &c.)
Wenching	*Verb*	Courting (Troilus and Cressida V.IV)
Werrit	*Verb*	To worry
Werrit	*Noun*	Ones who worries (too much)
Weskit	*Noun*	Waistcoat
Whimmy	*Adj*	Full of whims
Whosen	*Pron*	Whose

Glossary

Wicked-mon	*Noun*	The devil.
Wimbling	*Adj*	Of slender growth, particular of plants.
Yaux	*Verb*	To cough or expectorate
Yourn	*Pron*	Yours
Yud	*Noun*	The head
Yup	*Noun*	A heap
Yut	*Verb*	To eat

This glossary has been culled from a variety of sources including:

'A List of Words and Phrases occurring in Shakespeare's plays which though generally considered obsolete are still in use in parts of Warwickshire and Worcestershire,' in E.A.B. Barnard, *Notes and Queries*, vol.II, pp.200-203 (also p.245).

Jesse Salisbury, *A Glossary of Words and Phrases used in S.E. Worcestershire* (London: J. Salisbury, 1893). The more recent publication *Words of Old Worcestershire* (Kidderminster: Kenneth Tomkinson Limited, undated but say 1980s) is essentially a reprint of this earlier work.

Various bits and pieces such as *Copy of the Shorthand Writer's Notes of the Judgement and Evidence of the Trial of the Evesham Election Petition* (House of Commons, 21 June 1880) [wonderfully if surprisingly funny in parts]

Conversations with my father & family & friends.

www.ingramcontent.com/pod-product-compliance
Lightning Source LLC
Chambersburg PA
CBHW020650130626

46552CB00003B/1483